Ex

Limestone Lan ~~~upes
of the Peak District

by Trevor D Ford and John Gunn

assisted by Andrew Chamberlain,
David Judson and Tony Waltham

A Walking and Cycling Guide
BCRA Cave Studies Series 19

64pp, A5, 33 photos, 12 maps/drawings

PUBLISHER:
British Cave Research Association
The Old Methodist Chapel
Great Hucklow BUXTON SK17 8RG
enquiries@bcra.org.uk www.bcra.org.uk
U.K. Registered Charity: 267828

CAVE STUDIES SERIES EDITOR:
David Judson Hurst Barn Castlemorton
MALVERN WR13 6LS 01684 311057
cave-studies@bcra.org.uk

PRINTED BY:
Stoate & Bishop Printers Ltd
1 Shaftesbury Industrial Centre
The Runnings, CHELTENHAM
GL51 9NH 01242 236741
studio@stoateandbishop.com
www.stoateandbishop.com

FIRST EDITION

CONTENTS

ILLUSTRATIONS

ABOUT THE AUTHORS

Dr Trevor Ford OBE was, for many years, senior lecturer in geology at Leicester University. He is the leading expert on the geology, geomorphology and mineralogy of the White Peak area of Derbyshire, with many books written, or contributed to (*see Further Reading/Bibliography page 62-3).*

John Gunn is a Professor in the School of Geography, Earth and Environmental Sciences at Birmingham University, as well as being responsible for the running and co-ordination of the Limestone Research Group, also based there. John is an expert on the physical geography, geology and hydrology of the White Peak.

David Judson is a semi-retired architect, walker and cyclist who shapes and pulls together the Cave Studies Series for BCRA. He has written on cave related subjects in the past, but now mainly enjoys enriching these excursion guides and widening their appeal through a diverse interest base.

Andrew Chamberlain is Professor of Biological Anthropology at the University of Sheffield. He contributed Chapter 5, and has advised on all matters archaeological and/or palaeontological. He has investigated archaeological caves in South Devon, the Peak District and the Yorkshire Dales, and has made a special study of cave burials in Britain.

Dr Tony Waltham (a former Series Editor of this Series) has provided a broad overview and general guidance as well as making available his extensive photographic library for illustration purposes. Eleven of his photographs appear here.

ACKNOWLEDGEMENTS

Firstly we thank all of the contributing authors, David, Andrew and Tony for their assistance with this publication. We also thank Jerry Wooldridge for assisting with reproduction of all of the photographs, and especially for the creation of the drawings and the cover design. Photographs are credited on page three, but particular thanks are due to Lindsey Porter for Figure 35, on page 50, taken from his book, *Leek and Manifold Valley Light Railway* 2002 - *full reference page 63.* We also thank David Lowe for his meticulous and challenging comments on an early draft.

Trevor Ford and John Gunn 2010   ISBN: 978-0-900265-35-8

PREFACE

With Cave Studies 19 we are returning to one of the two central themes of this series of publications. Tony Waltham set the pace with No.1 "Caves & Karst of the Yorkshire Dales" back in 1987, and it was developed considerably with No.13 "Exploring the Limestone Landscapes of Upper Wharfedale" (2003), and " ... the Three Peaks and Malham" (2005). No.2 "Cave Surveying" (1988) started the other theme, good practice and technical advice for cavers, and this was updated by No.11 (effectively a Second Edition) in 2002 *see list on page 64.*

We returned to our first theme, guides interpreting our beautiful limestone scenery, perhaps more aimed at the non-caver than the dedicated caver, with No.3 "Caves & Karst of the Peak District" (1990). This is now out of print and a little dated, so that this current title picks up where that left off. The basic geology and geomorphology of "The White Peak" - its limestones, its caves and its mineralization, form the core of this publication, but following from the recently successful Nos. 13 and 15 ("Upper Wharfedale" and "The Three Peaks and Malham" - both in the Yorkshire Dales National Park), we have broadened our material to take in cave related archaeology and mineral extraction - metalliferous mining and quarrying.

As with the other titles of the interpretational theme we start with the basic geological and geomorphological fundamentals of the area. Here in the Peak District, there are to be found some of the most complex cave systems in Britain. The long geomorphological history is responsible for this. From the start of the deposition of the Carboniferous limestone itself, some 350M years ago, right up to the present day, caves have been in the process of development. This has been further complicated through several phases of volcanic activity and its associated mineralization.

Within the area, Castleton is one of the most visited honeypots, with its choice of Show Caves/Mines open to the general public. These range from the dramatic Peak Cavern, or "The Devil's Arse in the Peak", the unusual Speedwell Cavern, with its boat level, and the more modest but beautiful Treak Cliff Cavern and Blue John Cavern.

It is hardly surprising then that in and around here the most extensive 'wild' caves are also to be found. Peak and Speedwell Caverns and the amazing Titan Shaft *(cover photo)* have been linked to form 15km of sometimes tortuous interconnected cave system. Eldon Hole and Nettle Pot are challenging vertical features, and with Oxlow Caverns and other caves and mines also to the southwest of Castleton, this makes for an area of considerable caving activity.

With the exception offered by the several show caves (all indicated on the maps and mentioned in the text), we strongly advise readers that they should not enter any caves unless in the company of one or more experienced cavers.

Also, most of the sites mentioned here are situated on private land, and the wishes of the farmers, landowners or their occupiers must be respected. Mention herein does not imply a public right of way, although most of the recommended walks and/or cycle routes do have legal status, and these are shown on the excursion maps as appropriate.

David Judson   Series Editor.

Figure 1: Thorpe Cloud from the east with Hamston Hill in the foreground *photo: David Judson*

1 INTRODUCTION – CAVES and KARST

Forming the southern end of the Pennines, the Peak District is mostly within the county of Derbyshire, with a small southwestern area extending into Staffordshire. It has two distinct parts, the "Dark Peak", with its Millstone Grit moors and shale-floored valleys, substantially to the north but also along both west and east flanks, and the "White Peak" to the south, comprising limestone country with beautiful dales and caves.

This book is concerned only with the White Peak, which is some 40km from north to south and generally 10–15km wide. It rises to an altitude of around 450m above sea level, and is drained by the River Derwent and its tributaries to the east, and by the rivers Dove and Manifold to the west. All of these are tributaries of the Trent, which flows right around the area in a huge anticlockwise sweep.

Most of the White Peak lies within the Peak District National Park, established in 1951 and the first such park in Britain. However some areas were excluded on account of their high intensity of quarrying, which still continues. The towns of Buxton and Matlock, together with most of the lower Derwent Valley south of Rowsley are also just outside the Park boundary.

The White Peak is one of five British Carboniferous Limestone areas that display significant surface and underground karst landforms, the others being the Yorkshire Dales, the Mendip Hills, South Wales (including the Forest of Dean) and North Wales. These five areas have roughly comparable altitudes and similar climates, but their surface landforms and cave systems differ as a result of local variations in environments of rock deposition, tectonic history, glacial activity and cover deposits. For example, the White Peak lay beyond the limits of the most recent Pleistocene (Devensian) glacial advances and as a result the area has no extensive limestone pavements and only scattered remnant patches of boulder clay, left behind by earlier glaciations. There are also few vertical potholes such as those that are characteristic of the Yorkshire Dales, and no extensive sub-horizontal river caves comparable with those explored in South Wales.

A particular feature of the White Peak is the hydrothermal mineralization which is more intense than in most other British limestone areas. Mineral veins containing galena (lead ore), fluorite, baryte and calcite are widespread across the area. Consequently there are extensive mining remnants, with a very high density of abandoned shafts in some areas. Indeed, outside the Camborne–Redruth area of Cornwall there is no area of

6

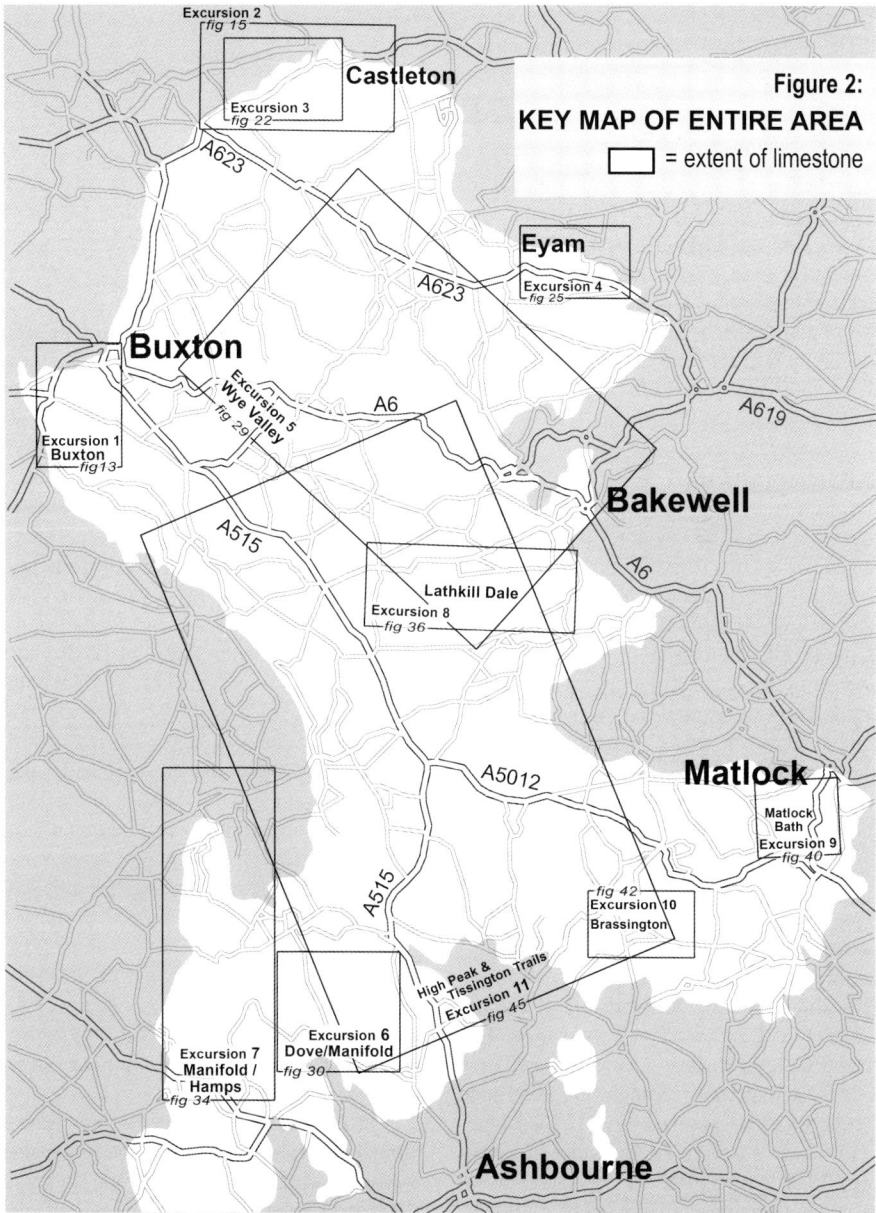

Figure 2:
KEY MAP OF ENTIRE AREA

☐ = extent of limestone

Excursion 2
fig 15

Castleton

Excursion 3
fig 22

A623

Eyam

Excursion 4
fig 25

A623

Buxton

Excursion 5
Wye Valley
fig 29

A6

A619

Excursion 1
Buxton
fig 13

Bakewell

A515

Lathkill Dale
Excursion 8
fig 36

A6

A5012

Matlock

Matlock
Bath
Excursion 9
fig 40

A515

fig 42
Excursion 10
Brassington

High Peak &
Tissington Trails
Excursion 11
fig 45

Excursion 7
Manifold /
Hamps
fig 34

Excursion 6
Dove/Manifold
fig 30

Ashbourne

Britain so densely affected by these potentially dangerous reminders of our mining heritage. The early lead miners were the first cavers – exploring natural cavities intersected by their mined passages.

Limestone quarrying is still extensive, and Tunstead Quarry near Buxton is one of the largest such undertakings in Europe. There are very few working mines, although re-working of surface spoil for fluorite and/or baryte still goes on in some areas.

---- ---- ~~~ ---- ----

2 GEOLOGY

The White Peak is composed mainly of limestones of early Carboniferous age. Some 500m of beds are exposed, and deep boreholes have proved the existence of at least another 1km in places, so that there is no impermeable basement at outcrop. Most of the limestones were deposited in shallow seas and are thus rich in fossils. The Carboniferous sea-floor also had a varied topography. A pattern of lagoons, reefs (= mud-mounds) ramps, fore-reef slopes and basin deposits has been identified. Both the landforms and the caves reflect the varied character of the limestones. In particular marginal reefs at Castleton, Upper Dovedale and around Matlock and Wirksworth form striking hills bordering the lagoonal limestones of the central plateau of the White Peak. Deep-water mud-mounds occur on the outer slopes of ramps in lower Dovedale. The Manifold Valley cuts through both deep-water mud-mounds and thin-bedded basinal limestones.

Alongside limestone deposition there was intermittent volcanic activity, and both lava flows and clouds of tuff or ash were erupted and deposited on limestone islands and on the sea floor, forming rock beds that are known locally as toadstones. Thinner layers of volcanic ash locally known as clay-wayboards, were also deposited and now occur sporadically through the limestone sequence. The permeability of toadstones and wayboards is lower than that of karstified limestone, and hence they have influenced the underground movement of mineralizing fluids and percolating rainwater at different times during the area's geological history.

At the end of the early Carboniferous episode of limestone sedimentation there were widespread earth movements resulting in folding of the limestone beds. With fold axes being mainly west–east in the eastern part of the White Peak, beds dip either north or south, and subterranean drainage tends to flow either down dip or along the strike. Some of these folds plunge eastwards so that drainage routes within them can be both down-dip and down plunge. In the western part of the White Peak the fold axes trend north–south, for example in the Manifold Valley, where underground drainage routes are complicated by the tight folding. The combination of facies changes in the limestone beds and the pattern of fold axes has contributed to the complexity of some cave patterns.

Renewed folding took place in late Carboniferous times, generally accentuating the previous folds and also affecting the thick cover strata of deltaic sands and muds, now forming the Millstone Grit and Coal Measures groups. A thickness of about 2km of these clastic sediments once lay on top of the limestone, but following later upwarping along the Pennine axis erosion has stripped off the cover and thus exhumed the limestone. The main features of the remnants of this cover are now to be seen as gritstone escarpments known locally as edges (Axe Edge, Black Edge, High Edge, etc) which provide a natural boundary around the White Peak.

Stresses associated with folding opened numerous fractures, which then became repositories for the hydrothermal mineral suite of galena, fluorite, baryte and calcite deposited from hot fluids rising from adjacent sedimentary basins. Mineralization occurred mainly in late Carboniferous times. Mineralizing fluids rose at temperatures between 70 and 120°C at a time when the entire area was still covered by the Millstone

Figure 3: Winnats Pass   *photo: Trevor Ford*

Grit and Coal Measures. The veins containing these minerals fall into several categories, (rakes, scrins, flats and pipes), and their surface traces are now marked by lines of old workings and waste heaps.

Some 15km² of the limestones in the southern part of the White Peak have been affected by dolomitization. This involves the conversion of calcite molecules into molecules of the double carbonate of calcium and magnesium. The process destroys fossils, increases porosity, and reduces rock solubility. The origin of the magnesium and the cause of the process are controversial, but dolomitization is now widely regarded as an early phase of mineralization. Locally the contact between dolomite and unaltered limestone has been the target of special forms of mineralization and the site of cave development, particularly in the Matlock and Brassington areas.

Following the erosional stripping of most of the Millstone Grit (and younger) cover, the later seas of the Permian period might have transgressed the South Pennines, but no deposits of Permian age survive. Rocks deposited during the succeeding Triassic period are represented by sandstones, pebbly sandstones and conglomerates, the remnants of which abut the limestone in a small area near Ashbourne.

Deposited in late Tertiary times (Miocene–Pliocene), the Brassington Formation consists of spreads of clays, sands and a few gravel layers derived from the nearby Triassic formations. The Brassington Formation once covered the greater part of the southern White Peak. Relics of the Formation have subsided into collapse-structures in the limestone, to form the so-called Pocket Deposits, well known around Brassington and around Newhaven to the northwest *see pages 58 and 61.*

Glaciers scoured the Peak District several times during the Pleistocene, the last time being around 480–425,000 years ago, during the Anglian Glaciation. However, the White Peak was ice free during the most recent (Devensian) glaciation so that glacial effects and deposits are less distinct than those in more recently glaciated area such as the Yorkshire Dales. Instead there are deposits that formed under periglacial conditions, which take the form of structureless masses of unsorted debris (head), fine sediment (loess) blown in by wind from the extensive glacial outwash deposits in adjacent areas, and widespread but localized scree deposits.

3 GEOMORPHOLOGY

The White Peak is essentially a soil-covered, gently undulating limestone plateau surface, ranging in altitude from 275–450m, and devoid of significant residual hills. This plateau surface is dissected by a complex network of sinuous valleys most of which are dry under present climatic conditions, and only two of which carry permanent surface streams – the Dove and Wye.

The dry valleys are thought to have developed on the Millstone Grit cover, and been superimposed onto the limestone as erosion lowered the surface. The development of conduits allowed increasing amounts of water to flow underground, leading to a gradual desiccation of the surface. In addition the driving of lead mine drainage levels (known as 'soughs' in the Peak District) has captured some of the remaining surface flow, most notably in the upper Lathkill. The dry valleys probably carried surface streams again during the Pleistocene cold periods, when permafrost inhibited underground drainage.

The other characteristic karst landforms are closed depressions (dolines) which pit the plateau surface. Dissolution and suffosion dolines are common, although analysis of their form and pattern has been complicated by the past activities of lead miners, by recent reworking of their waste hillocks for fluorspar, and by the practice of some farmers of infilling depressions to create level fields. Collapse dolines are less common although there are a few examples in the Castleton area. As the Peak District lay outside the limits of Devensian ice there is a virtually continuous soil cover with only a few areas of bare limestone and few karren features.

The central part of the White Peak is largely devoid of surface drainage, and water tracing experiments have shown that there is a well developed underground drainage system. However, most of this drainage is presumed to be through conduits that are too small for human access as only 50km of cave passage have been explored, much less than might be expected from about 540km^2 of limestone outcrop. Water is essential to cave development, and at present only the northern boundary of the limestone, and small areas to the west, abut topographically higher shales from which streams flow into the region's major cave systems. Elsewhere the limestones are generally higher than the sur-

Figure 4: The Stream Cave, Peak Cavern, a superb phreatic tube   *photo: J Wooldridge*

Figure 5:
The Bung Hole,
Speedwell Cavern
photo: Jerry Wooldridge

rounding land so there are now few streams to provide an input of water to dissolve the limestone. However, in the past the shale cover was more extensive and isolated segments of abandoned cave passage that are scattered beneath the area provide evidence that there were once more extensive cave systems. Some of these might have been removed by erosion as the limestone surface lowered, but the lack of presently accessible passage is in part because of pervasive mud deposits that limit exploration in many caves and probably obscure the entrances to others. Some of these muds are derived from relatively recent deposits of periglacial loess and solifluction material, but others have been shown to be over 700,000 years old, confirming that the caves in which they lie are even older. Indeed, Elderbush Cave in the Manifold Valley *see Excursion 7* has stalagmite deposits more than 1.7 million years old, so the cave must have reached its present size, and been drained, before then. It is likely that there are other equally ancient caves that are filled with sediment.

The impermeable basement rocks that are known at depth beneath the White Peak exercise little obvious influence on underground water movement, so deep phreatic circulation probably dominates in the area. It is this flow regime, and its undoubted links to the many mineral veins and the structures that originally fed them, that distinguishes the White Peak from the other British karst areas.

As mentioned above, in some areas the limestone has been altered to dolomite (the double carbonate of calcium and magnesium) *see Section 2*. Dolomitized limestones are less soluble but more porous, so they are more prone to physical weathering than are unaltered limestones, leaving behind masses of incoherent crystals that are known as dolomite sand or dolosand. Tors are characteristic landforms of the dolomite outcrops. Their origin has been a subject of considerable debate, with some authors arguing that their formation commenced in the Tertiary following deep chemical weathering, whereas others argue that the tors formed during the Quaternary cold periods when there was severe freeze-thaw activity.

4 CAVE DEVELOPMENT

Although the number of caves and length of cave passage are less than might be expected, caves of a great variety of morphological forms and evolutionary histories are to be found in the Peak District. The oldest are palaeokarstic caves associated with a mid-Carboniferous phase of uplift and karstification. At about 300M years old these are amongst the oldest cave remnants in Britain. During the mineralization phase the pipe-veins were effectively hydrothermal caves, initially enlarged due to dissolution by acidic waters during the Carboniferous period and subsequently partly filled or lined with minerals. Good examples are to be seen in Treak Cliff Cavern near Castleton and at Masson Hill, Matlock. Some of these have been modified by later meteoric drainage.

Much younger are the currently active stream caves, particularly those of the Castleton and Eyam-Stoney Middleton areas. The first stage of their development, their inception, probably occurred at depth whilst the limestones were still covered, but the formation of integrated conduit networks did not occur until the early phases of exposure of limestone by stripping off the cover of shales and sandstones. Some of the early conduits intersected previously isolated vein cavities, such as the Bottomless Pit in Speedwell Cavern, the great Oxlow Caverns and Leviathan and Titan in Far Peak Cavern.

Water circulation would initially have been very slow, with a rapid increase when the proto-conduits were intersected at lower levels by incising valleys on the edge of the newly exposed limestone massif. Initially, slow drainage dissolved out walls, floor and roof at the same rate giving rise to phreatic tube caves. Then water levels fell and allogenic streams entered these tubes, eroding their floors and carving canyon-like passages with classic 'keyhole' cross-sections.

Many passages in stream caves show a keyhole cross-section, with a phreatic tube in the roof and a still-active stream canyon in the floor. The allogenic inputs of water came from streams flowing off the Millstone Grit Group strata and sinking into swallets close to the shale/limestone margin. The overall form of a typical cave system around Castleton is a swallet draining into a canyon passage, and then through a series of mineral vein cavities, to emerge at a lower level, via sumps, at a resurgence cave or spring. The lower reaches of these resurgence caves might still be phreatic tubes, with variable degrees of canyon modification.

Many of the swallet caves enter the limestone in the reef belt, where cave development in the poorly bedded limestone has resulted in passages of variable size and shape. With the exception of areas that are beneath lava layers, most of the high-level relict cave passages are well decorated with stalactites and stalagmites (speleothems). These predominantly calcite deposits contain trace amounts of isotopes of uranium, and by measuring the quantity of certain isotopes it is possible to estimate the age of the speleothem and hence the minimum date at which the caves were drained. Using this evidence it is then possible to work out at least part of the evolutionary history of some cave systems.

---- ---- ~~~ ---- ----

Figure 6:
Sevenways Cave, near Wetton, Manifold Valley, from the cliff-top above Thor's Cave (next page) looking south-west. Elderbush Cave is close-by, behind the rock spur and trees on the right
photo: Andrew Chamberlain

5 CAVE ARCHAEOLOGY + PALAEONTOLOGY

Explorations in many White Peak caves have revealed archaeological and palaeontological remains constituting a diverse and important record of human cultures and their environments going back to the last ice age. Contrary to popular ideas, only a few of these caves would have been suitable for long-term occupation. Peak Cavern is the exception. Others, such as Hermit's Cave at Cratcliff Rocks near Birchover, may have been occupied by individuals seeking solitude.

Evidence suggests caves provided locations suitable for temporary or episodic events. They were used for refuge, for ceremonial activities including rites of burial, for storing or caching materials for future retrieval, and for brief periods of occupation during pastoral activities or hunting trips. Although many of these activities might have been ephemeral, the evidence from them is of great importance because caves help to provide missing information relating to past uses of the landscape. As the hunter-gatherers of the last ice age, were highly mobile peoples with no permanent settlements, much of our archaeological evidence has been recovered from excavations in caves.

HISTORY OF STUDY

Archaeological interest in the caves of the Peak District was stimulated by discoveries made by lead miners, quarry workers and navvies who encountered ancient remains when concealed caves were intersected by the excavation of mine shafts, adits, and railway cuttings. An early example was reported by Roger Gale in the Philosophical Transactions of the Royal Society in 1745, after a fossilised human skeleton was found in tufa during the driving of the Lathkill Dale Sough.

Following the publication of *Reliquiae Diluvianae* (relics of the flood) by Wm Buckland in 1823 the fight was on to prove

that the great flood, as recorded in the bible, was not really 'the big picture' but that cave entrances were receptacles of changing landscapes and developing human and animal environs over a much longer timescale.

With rapidly accumulating evidence for the great antiquity of humankind, interest in archaeological finds in caves intensified. The scientific excavation of cave deposits provided a means of showing that before and during the Pleistocene ice ages ancient humans had lived alongside animals that are now extinct.

Of the many who contributed to the archaeological investigation of the caves of the White Peak during the 19th and 20th centuries three stand out as playing key roles: Wm Boyd Dawkins in the late 19th century; J.Wilfred Jackson in the early 20th century and Don Bramwell in the second half of the 20th century. Boyd Dawkins included accounts of several important bone caves of the White Peak in *Cave Hunting* (1874), a book that greatly stimulated the nascent science of speleology. In 1953 Jackson wrote a national review of cave archaeology in which he summarised finds from 36 Peak District caves (revised

Figure 7: Thor's Cave, near Wetton, Manifold Valley - *see also Excursion 7* - a phreatic remnant cave now left high and dry some 70 metres above the river, a rich source of human/animal remains from the Pleistocene to Romano-British periods   *photo: Andrew Chamberlain*

as *Jackson 1962)*. Bramwell (1977) undertook the most comprehensive survey to date, providing details of 44 archaeological and palaeontological caves in the White Peak.

A recent research project, sponsored by English Heritage and carried out by a team from the universities of Sheffield and Bradford, reviewed all previous discoveries in the caves of the White Peak. The project determined that 45 of the caves were recorded as having contained archaeological remains, and a further 15 contained natural assemblages of animal bones, many of these being of ancient rather than modern origin. New discoveries of bones and artefacts continue to be made in the region's caves, and in nearly all cases these arise as accidental finds made by recreational cavers, though a few prospective excavations have been undertaken in recent years by academic archaeologists.

ARCHAEOLOGY & PALAEONTOLOGY

Finds in the caves of the White Peak include material spanning the long period from the early Pleistocene, possibly as old as 750,000 years, to the present day. Relatively few caves contain material from before 100,000 years ago, perhaps reflecting the fact that karst regions are geomorphologically active environments that are subject to continual

processes of erosion, cave breakdown and flushing through of sediments. Together these processes militate against the long-term survival of archaeological and palaeontological remains, especially those deposited near cave entrances. About a dozen Peak District caves have been shown to have been visited by Upper Palaeolithic peoples (from 40,000 to 10,000 years ago) as evidenced by finds of flaked stone and worked bone tools. Most evidence is from the post-glacial period of prehistory, 10,000 to 2,000 years ago.

Human skeletal remains are amongst the most common finds, and although their presence in caves might evoke sinister interpretations, the emerging consensus is that many caves were used as places of burial by the earliest farmers of the Neolithic (New Stone Age) and Bronze Age, 6,000 to 3,000 years ago. Some caves, such as Ravencliffe Cave in Cressbrook Dale and Carsington Pasture Cave, Brassington *see Excursion 10*, contained large quantities of human remains and clearly these sites rivalled chambered tombs as 'burial places' in Neolithic times. Many of these locations are prominent and/or elevated points in the landscape, such as Fox Hole Cave on High Wheeldon, and Thor's Cave, high in the cliff that dominates the upper section of the Manifold Valley.

Similar locations on hilltops and ridge crests were often chosen for burial mounds in the Neolithic and Bronze Age, perhaps with the belief that the ancestors would watch over the living in the valleys below?

Finds dating to the Romano-British period are also common, with remains typically including pottery, coins, bone implements and metal decorative artefacts. Many of these items are likely to be votive deposits rather than evidence of occupation, with caves serving as shrines where offerings were made to native deities. Mediaeval finds are rare, perhaps because with the arrival of Christianity there was active discouragement of ritual practices in caves.

REPORTING FINDS and LOCATING INFORMATION

Archaeological finds in caves belong to the landowner, but there is a legal obligation to report to the local coroner all discoveries of archaeological objects that contain precious metals and/or qualify as 'hoards', i.e. groups of coins or collections of prehistoric metal objects that were deposited together. In practice, it is sensible to report all finds of ancient artefacts to the Finds Liaison Officers, who work for the Portable Antiquities Scheme and are based at major regional museums: contact details are available at *www.finds.org.uk.* Important finds of a non-artefactual nature, such as human bones or bones of extinct animals, should be reported to the appropriate county or district archaeology service, which is usually based within the planning/environment sections of the local authority. National Parks have their own archaeology staff and discoveries within a Park should be reported to them.

Major collections of finds from the caves of the White Peak can be found in nearby museums, including Buxton (where there is an excellent display based on the work of Boyd Dawkins), Stoke-on-Trent, Derby and Sheffield. Information about many of the archaeological caves of Derbyshire and Staffordshire can be searched for on English Heritage's National Monuments Record, which is available online at *www.pastscape.org*

CRESWELL CRAGS VISITOR CENTRE

Although not strictly within the Peak District, but on the very eastern edge of Derbyshire, the caves, and their deposits, of the southern Magnesian Limestone outcrop cannot be omitted from a regional review such as this. A grant of £4.2M from the Heritage Lottery Fund has aided the development of a new educational visitor centre at Creswell Crags, located about 7km east of J30 on the M1.

As outlined in the previous section, the White Peak has revealed a broad spectrum of archaeological/palaeontological remains over the past 200 years or so of its investigation. The relationship between what has, and still is, being learnt further east and the possibly more thoroughly investigated caves of the Carboniferous upland area that is the White Peak is a long way from being fully understood. However, it is becoming increasingly clear that these lower and considerably more sheltered environs played a vital part in the recolonisation of Britain by hunter-gatherers during the retreat stages of the last Ice Age.

The small caves of the Creswell Gorge, and the other similar locations north and south of it, whilst of little interest to the average caver, are of great archaeological importance. In 2003 the first Palaeolithic cave art in Britain was discovered in Church Hole and further art has been found in other caves in the Cresswell Gorge. The new visitor centre is now a uniquely valuable resource in interpreting the finds and sreading the knowledge arising from them. (DMJ)

6 MINERAL EXTRACTION – MINING

The White Peak has been an important source of lead, zinc and copper ores, as well as the gangue minerals, fluorite, baryte and calcite, since before the Roman occupation. Lead ore in particular has been mined since Roman times, whilst a little copper ore was certainly produced at Ecton as far back as the Bronze Age. Although lead mining has long been uneconomical in the UK, fluorite, baryte and calcite are still in demand for industrial purposes and a few large open-pit mines remain in operation. Lead ore is a by-product in some instances.

Ore minerals have been found in several types of veins, notably rakes, scrins, flats and pipes. The first two are respectively large and small fissure fillings. They are generally more or less vertical features, commonly extending across country for up to several kilometres. Flats tend to follow the strata, and in the Peak District most are horizontal, or nearly so, and many are capped or floored by volcanic horizons. Pipes comprise minerals infilling linear cavities, some of which are of palaeokarstic origin, whilst others are related to breaks in sedimentation, or to unconformities. Some small areas of replacement deposits are also present, wherein the ore minerals, particularly fluorite, have replaced the limestone in irregular masses.

Some 2,000 named mineral veins have been worked across the Peak District, primarily for the lead ore, galena, with the greatest concentration in the eastern half of the area. The courses of the worked veins are now marked by lines of waste hillocks, many with concealed, collapsed or filled-in shafts. Some of the latter resemble dolines, but the raised waste heaps around them confirm their true origin.

Estimates of the total number of individual shafts range from 50,000 to 100,000. Many have been regarded as hazards, both for walkers and for farm animals, and have been capped by one means or another. In some cases a sound structural job has been achieved, but

Figure 8: Magpie Sough tail in winter   *photo: Tony Waltham*

more often it has been a matter of what comes to hand – for example concrete or timber railway sleepers.

The Countryside and Rights of Way Act 2000 (CRoW) has opened up considerable tracts of land to the public in both the White and the Dark Peak and the presence of open, or insecurely covered shafts has become a source of considerable concern to some landowners. All visitors should be aware of the potential dangers from open, poorly covered and concealed shafts and exercise extreme caution in this respect.

With so many abandoned mine workings, it is not surprising that the hillocks and shafts are a salient feature of the karst landscape, and prominent lines can be seen across many parts of the plateau. Many mines broke into natural caves by accident, and several of Castleton's largest cave systems were first entered in this way. The magnificent Speedwell Cavern stream caves, and the Oxlow Caverns, might have remained undiscovered if lead miners had not first broken into them. Some of the caves mentioned in this booklet can still only be entered via old mine workings.

Over time mines became deeper, and encountered drainage problems. From the 17th century onwards it became increasingly necessary to drive drainage levels – locally known as soughs. Over 100 of these soughs are recorded, a few being several kilometres long and with catchments of up to 50km^2. Soughs commonly had a substantial and lasting effect on

the water table, which was lowered considerably, locally revealing caves that would otherwise still be deep in the phreatic zone. The Blende Vein Cavern intersected by Magpie Sough beneath Sheldon, is a good example.

Regrettably only a few of these soughs are still accessible, but some are used as private or public water supplies. The generally non-filtering nature of limestone aquifers means that pollutants accidentally or deliberately left on the surface, dropped down mine shafts or deposited in dolines are likely to cause water supply pollution problems.

Other minerals have also been mined in particular areas of the Peak District. There are several kilometres of abandoned chert mine workings around Bakewell, and wad (manganese dioxide) was produced from several mines and caves around Winster. Iron ore in the form of earthy haematite has been mined near Hartington.

Figure 9: The Whirlpool, Speedwell Cavern
photo: Paul Deakin.

Figure 10: ELDON HILL during limestone quarrying, a blot on the landscape? Looking south from the A625 *(1988)* *photo: Tony Waltham*

7 MINERAL EXTRACTION – QUARRYING

Being within easy reach of six major conurbations, the Peak District's limestones are in high demand for aggregate, cement manufacture, and a host of other industrial purposes. Currently the White Peak, taken as a whole, is the largest supplier in Britain of limestone, or limestone derived materials, and contains one of the largest working limestone quarries – Tunstead.

The other large limestone quarries are Dove Holes, and the A515 quarries: Hillhead, Brierlow, Hindlow and Dowlow. These last three, when viewed from the Grinlow Tower on the outskirts of Buxton to the northwest, present a quite staggering image of landscape modifiction and destruction that is in marked contrast to the natural landscape in the nearby National Park *see Excursion 1.*

Of course the establishment of these quarries pre-dated the creation of the National Park and because of their importance as a source of limestone, and of employment, the Park boundary was drawn to exclude them.

Other large quarries are located at Hope, serving the cement factory, with its own purpose built rail-connection, Stoney Middleton, Caulden, Brassington, and a cluster (Dene, Middle Peak and others)

around Wirksworth near the southeastern extremity of the outcrop. A number of disused quarries on the northern edge of Wirksworth are now being utilised for light industry, and as the National Stone Centre – a visitor attraction that is sponsored partly by the stone industry.

There are now far fewer limestone quarries in the White Peak than was once the case. The smallest ones became uneconomical and some of the middle sized ones were closed when they reached the boundary of their existing consents and were unable to obtain planning permission for further expansion. Eldon Hill Quarry, which closed in 2005, is a good example. This was not a particularly large quarry, but it was eating away at the northern flank of the Hill, with a main face that was increasing in height and becoming more and more prominent. There were also concerns over impacts on the Castleton caves *see Excursion 2.*

Although much of the Peak District falls within the National Park, mineral production is a national economic requirement and a balance must be struck by the National Park Authority between extraction, conservation and recreational interests. This will never be an easy task.

---- ---- ~~ ---- ----

8
PUBLIC SHOW CAVES

Figure 11:
The Bottomless Pit,
Speedwell Cavern
photo:
Jerry Wooldridge

The White Peak has eight show caves/ mines that are open to the public, four in Castleton, one in Buxton and three in Matlock Bath. The caverns show important contrasts in their nature and mode of development. The Peak and Speedwell Caverns *Castleton, Excursion 2* and Poole's Cavern *Buxton, Excursion 1* are in part active, with streams in them, whereas Blue John Cavern and Treak Cliff Cavern (Castleton) and the Masson Cavern, Matlock Bath, *Excursion 9* are relict systems, abandoned by their main underground drainage long ago. Despite its name, the Rutland Cavern, Matlock Bath, *Excursion 9,* consists largely of mined passage. Temple Mine is also largely mined, but the workings extend into sand filled natural caverns. All should be visited to gain a clear picture of the subterranean aspects of this karst limestone area. *See Map, Figure 15 on page 25 for detailed locations of the four Show Caves in the Castleton area.*

Figure 12: Far Canal, Speedwell Cavern
photo: Jerry Wooldridge

9 EXCURSIONS

EXCURSION 1: BUXTON AREA WALKS 1.5 to 7.7km

Buxton, known to the Romans as Aquae Arnemetiae, lies in a topographic basin on the northwestern margin of the White Peak limestone area, with the gritstone ridges of Axe Edge 551m, Burbage Edge 500m and Black Edge 507m to the north and west. It has long been famous for its thermal springs (27°C), which are at least in part karstic. Although deep-seated in their origins, they finally rise through limestone strata. Studies of the chemistry of these thermal waters indicate that they circulate deep underground for around 5,000 years. Buxton also has a fine public Show Cave, Poole's Cavern, situated just off Green Lane on the southwestern edge of the town. The thermal springs and the old baths in Buxton's Crescent were closed to the public some years ago but the reputedly therapeutic waters can be sampled at St. Anne's Well on the opposite side of the road (SK 058 735) or in the modern swimming pool in the nearby Pavilion Gardens. Some of the thermal spring water is bottled and sold as "Buxton Water".

Poole's Cavern is well sign-posted (brown visitor information signs) from most parts of Buxton. It has a large car park, and in addition to the show cave and Visitor Centre there is also the Grinlow Woods Country Park, all owned by the Buxton Civic Association. There is thus visitor interest here in all weathers, and for most people with an interest in the natural environment.

We suggest that you start this excursion from the Poole's Cavern car park **1**, from which there are a number of worthwhile options ranging from 2km to almost 8km for the full circuit.

POOLE'S CAVERN

When it was first 'officially' opened to visitors in the 1850s this 240m-long tourist cave had already been known for several hundred years during which time it had received many famous visitors. One of the earliest was Mary Queen of Scots who is said to have visited in 1582 and to have leaned for support against a large flowstone mass that is now called the Mary Queen of Scots Pillar. The cavern is thought to have been named over a hundred years earlier after an outlaw who hid there in the fifteenth century, and Charles Cotton, in his *The Wonders of the Peak* (1683) wrote: *The first* [wonder]

I met in my way is a vast cave, in which the old people say, one Poole an outlaw made his residence.

Before the 1850s visitors entered the cave by crawling for around 10m to the first chamber. The enlargement process involved blasting off part of the low roof and the removal of large amounts of sediment that was found to contain human and animal bones. In the 1860s further excavations beneath a layer of stalagmite within the cave revealed animal and human remains plus some Roman coins, pottery and a bronze brooch inlaid with silver. Signs of the most recent excavations, undertaken during the 1980s and 1990s, are visible in the so-called Roman Chamber just inside the entrance.

Initially illuminated by candles, Poole's was one of the first caves to be illuminated by town gas, installed by its then owner, the 6th Duke of Devonshire in 1859. Some of the gas fittings still remain, although the system was replaced with a conventional electric one when the cave was re-opened in 1976.

Poole's Cavern is situated on the north flank of the Grin Low Anticline, with a catchment extending to the area around the former Stanley Moor reservoir **6**. It must once have been the main resurgence for the

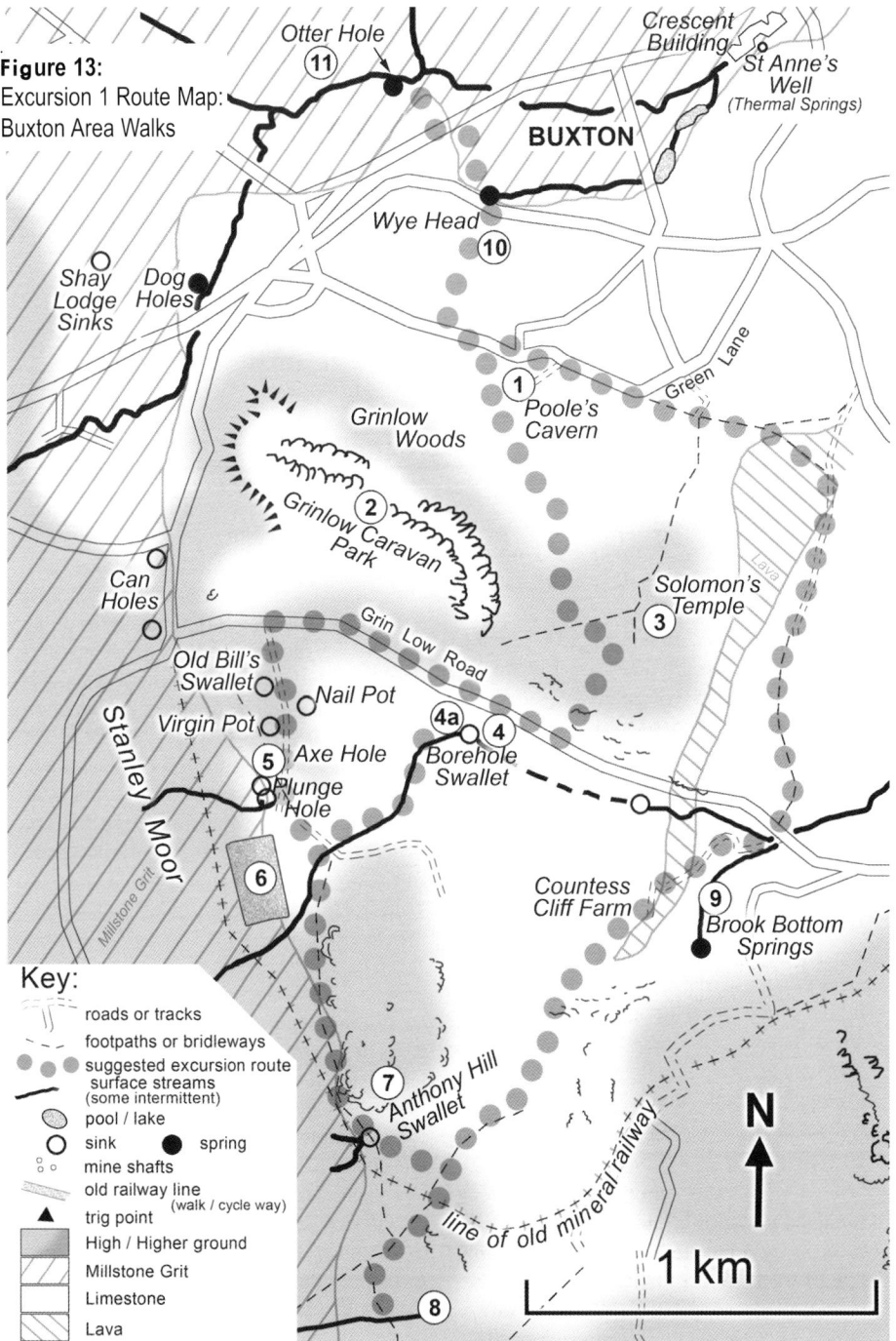

Figure 13:
Excursion 1 Route Map:
Buxton Area Walks

Otter Hole
(11)

Crescent Building
St Anne's Well
(Thermal Springs)

BUXTON

Wye Head
(10)

Shay Lodge Sinks
Dog Holes

Grinlow Woods
(1) Poole's Cavern
Green Lane

(2) Grinlow Caravan Park
Lava

Can Holes

Solomon's Temple
(3)

Old Bill's Swallet
Nail Pot
Virgin Pot
Grin Low Road

(4a) (4) Borehole Swallet

(5) Axe Hole
Plunge Hole

Stanley Moor

Millstone Grit

(6)

Countess Cliff Farm

(9) Brook Bottom Springs

Key:

roads or tracks
footpaths or bridleways
suggested excursion route
surface streams (some intermittent)
pool / lake
sink   spring
mine shafts
old railway line (walk / cycle way)
trig point
High / Higher ground
Millstone Grit
Limestone
Lava

(7) Anthony Hill Swallet

line of old mineral railway

N

1 km

(8)

21

area, but the majority of the drainage now by-passes it and travels through inaccessible conduits to the Wye Head and Otter Hole resurgences. Most of the cave is a large vadose stream passage with abundant speleothems; the stream drains down-dip towards the dry entrance but sinks in the floor before reaching it. The accessible cave ends abruptly upstream at a large boulder choke, partly cemented by stalagmite. Considerable digging effort here has so far failed to find a way through, but in 1998 a survey using ground penetrating radar suggested that there is open cave passage beyond and this was later proved by a series of boreholes.

Some of the speleothems in Poole's Cavern are of interest because of their rapid growth and orange coloration which means they resemble the appearance of poached eggs. The presence of stalagmites on top of Victorian gas pipe provides visual evidence of the speed of growth and rates of up to 5mm per year have been measured, over 50 times faster than would normally be expected in a Peak District cave. The reason for the rapid growth is the presence of waste deposits from former lime-burning kilns in the woods above the cave (see below). Water passing through these slaked lime deposits takes the calcium hydroxide into solution and when the water emerges in the cave there is rapid absorption of carbon dioxide from the cave air and precipitation of calcium carbonate. This is the opposite of the common process of speleothem deposition in which carbon dioxide is lost from the water causing it to become saturated and to precipitate calcium carbonate.

THE WALK

From the top of the car park (away from the cave entrance) there are signs to Buxton Country Park (Grin Plantation), and to the nearby caravan park **2** and Solomon's Temple **3**. The area now occupied by appar-

Figure 14: Poole's Cavern *photo: Tony Waltham*

ently native woodland was an industrial area from the 16th to the 19th centuries. Limestone was quarried and burnt in "pudding pie" kilns to produce lime which was used as a fertiliser and as mortar. The waste from this activity was dumped on the hillside and has subsequently had a profound effect on stalagmites in Poole's Cavern. Reclamation began in the 1820s when the Duke of Devonshire responded to complaints about the appearance of the area by ordering trees to be planted. These now form 40 hectares of mature woodland, the main species being Beech, Ash, Elm and Sycamore with Willow, Birch, Hawthorn and Rowen around the edges.

The direct ascent towards Solomon's Temple is via a set of steep steps, but there is also a range of less-steep meandering paths heading up the hillside. It is best to follow a path that trends to the left as those to the right lead to a safety fence around the former Grinlow Quarry. Some 20 years ago the quarry was laid out as a spacious and well-landscaped caravan park that is largely out of view, an excellent example of after-use. Parts of the quarry lie very close indeed to the end of Poole's Cavern. So much so that when coal was temporarily stored in the quarry in the 1950s black coal-dust got washed through into the Cavern, and right through to Wye Head. It is said that one of the thermal springs was also affected. If you wish to visit the quarry then follow the path to the west after leaving the woodland and crossing into an open grassy area.

At the southeast corner of the Wood footpaths from two exits cross open grassland to the high-point (437m) of the small limestone hill that is surmounted by the Grinlow Tower **3**, or Solomon's Temple as it is better known. This is a Victorian folly built in 1896 to replace an earlier structure constructed by Solomon Mycock, a local farmer and landowner, and restored in 1988.

On reaching the ridge the first long-view is to the southeast, dominated by limestone quarries and their various processing plants. The short ascent of the Tower is well worthwhile, because from here the views to the north suddenly open-up, right across the whole town of Buxton, whereas to the south and southwest there are views across Stanley Moor to Leap Edge and Axe Edge.

After the Tower there are a number of options – the longest circuit (7.7km) takes you initially south through the obvious stile close below the Tower. There are also at least two shorter routes heading north or northwest. These take you back to Poole's Cavern, through Grin Plantation, either direct to the car park or via Green Lane. From the stile the path descends steeply to Grin Low Road. Follow this right for 900m and then take the track left towards the former reservoir **6**. This was never fully operational because, due to its location on the shale/limestone junction it suffered persistent leakage, and was finally taken out of use during the 1990s.

As elsewhere in the Peak District, streams that have their origins on the shales and sandstones of the surrounding Millstone Grit Group sink a short distance after crossing on to the limestone and are augmented by percolation water before emerging at several springs. All of the waters ultimately drain to the River Wye but the underground hydrology is complex and still not fully understood.

Some of the many closed depressions that pit the surrounding moor are suffosion dolines (shakeholes) but other pits are the result of lead mining activities. The building visible in a dry valley to the south of the road houses the now disused Ladmanlow borehole **4**, drilled to 177m depth, all in limestone. When pumped, this altered the underground drainage patterns and reduced the stream in Poole's Cavern almost to nil. However it is no longer in use and the pump has been removed.

Situated close to the faulted shale/limestone margin, Axe Hole and Plunge Hole **5**, are adjacent stream sinks that have developed on joints parallel to the main fault. A sizeable stream sinks at Plunge Hole but the cave ends in a sump in a narrow rift after only 15m. Axe Hole has a smaller stream but a greater length of passage. The two streams drain primarily to both Otter Hole and Wye Head Resurgences (the latter partly via Poole's Cavern except in low flow) but water tracing has also demonstrated a link to Brook Bottom Springs **9**.

One of the streams that has its origins on Leap Edge is channelled round the reservoir and sinks in its bed at several points to the south of the public footpath, the final one being Borehole Swallet **4a**. Unlike the drainage from Axe Hole and Plunge Hole this water flows only to Wye Head, part of the flow passing through Poole's Cavern in all but the lowest of discharges. The valley below the main sink is dry, except in flood conditions.

Another small stream sinks close to the shale margin at Anthony Hill Swallet **7**. The majority of flow from here is towards the Brook Bottom Springs **9**, but some also drains to Otter Hole and Wye Head. All of the water from Leap Edge Swallet **8**, and parts of the waters from Axe Hole, Plunge Hole and Anthony Hill Swallet resurge in the valley below Countess Cliff. The original site or sites have been obscured by the tipping of quicklime waste through which the water emerges in several places. Just as in the Poached Egg Chamber of Poole's Cavern, the reaction of the quicklime (calcium oxide) with carbon dioxide (in the water and air) produces calcium carbonate and there are spectacular tufa deposits in the source area together with smaller dams along the course of the stream down to the River Wye at Lovers' Leap (in Ashwood Dale on the edge of Buxton). Studies have shown that in the source area over 1m depth of tufa has accumulated in around 100 years.

Heading back, from Countess Cliff Farm, re-cross Grin Low Road, left then right, and the footpath takes you along the back of Fern House. Before joining the A515 take the left fork and cut across to Green Lane via the school playing fields.

THE SOURCES OF THE RIVER WYE
Short Walk to Wye Head 1.5km

From Poole's Cavern a separate excursion can be made to the Wye Head Springs **10**. After leaving the car park cross Green Lane and follow it up hill for about 200 metres until you meet a narrow footpath between houses. Follow this down hill and through a housing estate to another narrow footpath which emreges onto a main highway, Macclesfield Road. The springs, which are directly opposite on the other side of the road, are generally held to be the source of the River Wye. However, a comparably large quantity of water is discharged from the nearby Otter Hole resurgence **11**, some 400m to the northwest. To visit this site follow the footpath that starts on the west side of Wye Head until it reaches the A53. Turn left and follow the road for 200m until you reach a new housing development on the north side of the road. Follow the main road through the estate to Otter Hole which has been retained as a water feature. Returning to the A53 follow the road uphill to Burbage, turn left, cross the first road and then either follow the minor road back to Poole's cavern or take one of the paths through Grin Plantation.

Otter Hole Resurgence and the Wye Head Springs have a shared catchment area, are situated near the limestone/shale junction and are probably relatively recent features, since the Wye Head Springs come from impenetrable fissures and Otter Hole has only 36m of tight, immature, accessible passage. From these small beginnings the River Wye flows right across the northern part of the White Peak, eventually joining the River Derwent at Rowsley beyond Bakewell. For interesting viewpoints *see Excursion 5*

EXCURSION 2:
THE CASTLETON KARST
Cycle Ride: 16-17km

The recommended start point **1** is just above the Blue John Cavern **2** at the western end of the minor road that was formerly the A625 from Chapel-en-le-Frith to Sheffield. This is as far as the old main road can now be followed by car as it was closed in 1979 after having been truncated by a landslip. We suggest a visit to this fascinating physical feature on your way back from Castleton (see below). A visit to Blue John Cavern can be made now, or at the end of your journey.

2   BLUE JOHN CAVERN
The Cavern is entered via a staircase excavated by 18th century miners. This leads into an extensive system of phreatic caves modi-

fied by vadose canyons of which less than half are visited on the public tour.

The first section near the surface is a short series of phreatic passages with Blue John fluorspar workings leading off and believed to be the Waterhull Pipe, first worked in 1709. Originally visitors were taken down a ladderway in a narrow pothole, but a stairway and ramps bypass was installed about 1836. This led to a tributary stream passage and more Blue John workings. It joined the large vadose canyon at the Crystallized Cavern. From here to the end of the public section the path follows a magnificent canyon passage up to 25m high and 5m wide. This leads into Lord Mulgrave's Dining Room, which shows extensive phreatic development in the roof. A low branch leads into Blue John workings leading to Stemple Cavern and the Fairy Grotto with its stalactite decorations.

At the end of the public section the Variegated Cavern is some 30m high and, shortly beyond the barrier, it is joined by a tribu-

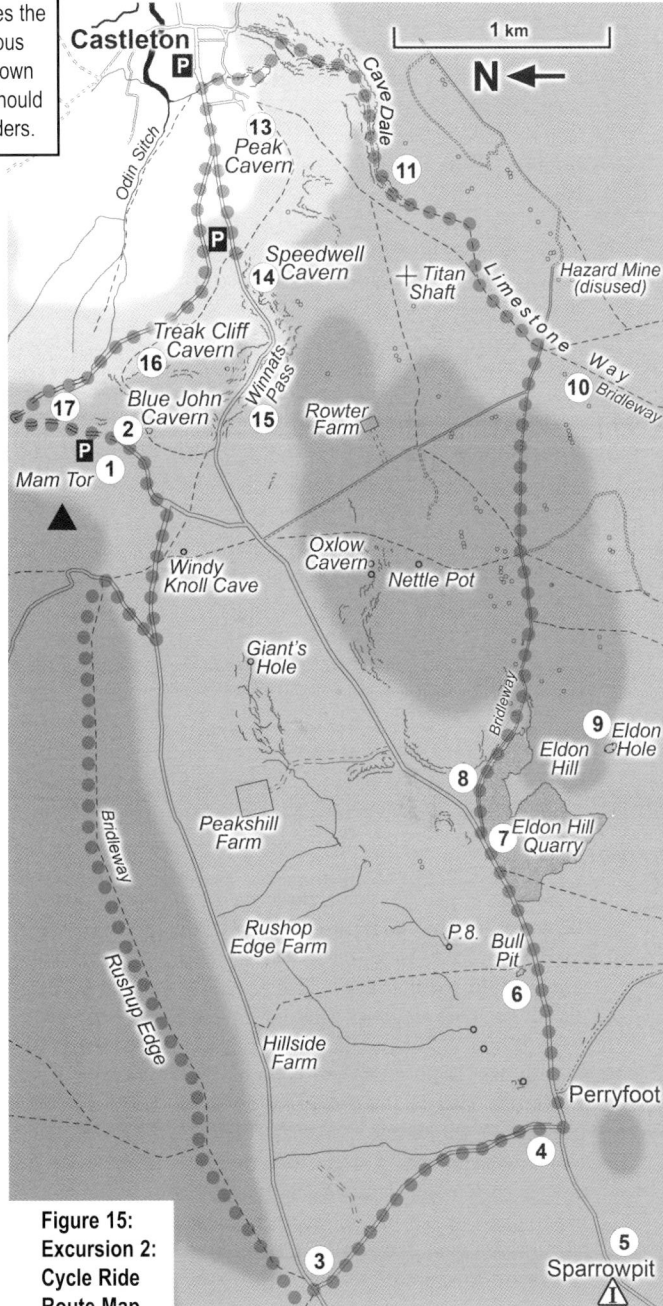

Figure 15: Excursion 2: Cycle Ride Route Map

tary canyon – the Inferior Gallery. Together these descend rapidly to a final chamber. The size of these canyon passages indicates enlargement of a phreatic tube by a former major free-surface stream, presumably draining off the slopes of an ancestral Mam Tor.

In the earlier phreatic phase of dissolution slow-moving waters were ponded up by Millstone Grit shales before the Hope Valley had been eroded to its present level. Such waters appear to have made use of pre-existing weaknesses in the limestone in the form of mineral pipe veins containing Blue John, a variety of fluorspar – mined from the cavern walls in several places. These pipe veins suggest that a palaeokarst, including underground drains, of mid-Carboniferous age existed before mineralization took place.

The small stream present in the Blue John Cavern today is a misfit, which was not responsible for the erosion of the canyon. This water emerges in Castleton from Russet Well and Slop Moll (see below).

THE EXCURSION

Follow the minor road (former A625) back towards Chapel-en-le-Frith and after 1km turn right, signposted Barber Booth and Edale. There is a short steep ascent to a dramatic windy col. The steep end of the Mam Tor ridge is now directly ahead, but turn back again here to a further short, steep ascent of the Rushup Edge. This rough bridleway tops the summit of the Edge (Lords Seat) at 542m, before descending gently back to the road at its highest point.

From most of this ridgeway there are fine views across the Perryfoot drainage basin, to the immediate south, an area of significant speleological interest. In the shallow basin there is a line of swallets where streams draining the shale and sandstone slopes of Rushup Edge disappear underground shortly after crossing onto the limestone. The waters from all of these sinks and caves (e.g. Giants Hole), eventually pass beneath the surface watershed to reappear at Castleton. Each stream flows in a channel incised into a sheet of periglacial solifluction deposits consisting largely of sandstone pebbles derived from Rushup Edge. The watershed is also traversed by many mineral veins, several containing deep vein cavities that have been extensively mined. The view is dominated by Eldon Hill and its quarry, which closed in the 1990s when its planning consent expired.

Shortly after re-joining the former A625 turn left **3**. and descend the narrow lane to Perryfoot and a T junction with a larger road. Just before the junction look to your right and you will see a stream that sinks at the base of a cliff (P1 Swallet) **4**. Two adjacent but unconnected caves have been explored here, Perryfoot Cave and Dr Jackson's Cave. Both are only a few hundred metres in length with tight complicated passages leading to sumps. Permission to visit should be obtained from Tor Top Farm.

The water from the two caves, and from P0 Swallet to the west, flows via the workings of the old Coalpithole Mine (lead) and re-appears some 5km to the east at Russet Well and Slop Moll in Castleton. In Coalpithole Mine the waters disappear into a sump, which the miners referred to as a "great swallow". A survey of the mine shows that the sump is at almost the same altitude as the Main Rising in Speedwell Cavern, demonstrating the presence of a long phreatic vein cavity system beneath the intervening 3km of ground.

Going right at the Perryfoot junction, the main A623 Chapel en le Frith – Peak Forest road and the Wanted Inn are just 1km away **5** and the most westerly swallet in the Castleton drainage system, P0, lies to the north of this road.

Going left at the junction takes you

Figure 16: Looking down Cave Dale
with Peveril Castle on the left
photo: Tony Waltham

back towards Castleton and after 800m you will pass a Public Footpath on your left that leads past the Bull Pit **6**. This is a 25m-deep collapse doline with somewhat degraded sides. Although several attempts have been made to dig a way into the cave into which it presumably collapsed, none has yet been successful.

A short distance further on you will pass the site of the former Eldon Hill Quarry **7** on your right. There is little evidence of the buildings that marked this recently active quarry but the quarry face remains as a scar on the side of Eldon Hill.

After passing the former quarry workings turn right onto a bridleway that follows around the eastern flank of the Quarry **8**. This makes an easy ascent close to the old quarry. You can observe here the working methods, whereby the main face (the north face) has up to five steps (benches) at its highest point (about 40m). At present this disused quarry is a sterile space, but there are possible after-uses *see Grinlow Quarry, Excursion 1.*

The summit of Eldon Hill is 470m above sea level, the highest exposure of limestone in the Peak District. About 300m

to the south, on private land, lies perhaps the second most historically famous speleological feature of the White Peak – Eldon Hole **9**. This is the only large deep open pothole in the Peak, and being such a rare challenge it was a magnet for the early 'potholers', along with Gaping Gill and Alum Pot in Yorkshire. Eldon Hole was bottomed by J. Lloyd in 1770, Alum Pot by John Birkbeck in 1870, and finally Gaping Gill by Eduard Martel in 1895. However, it is alleged that the first to reach the bottom of Eldon Hole was a man who was lowered on a rope around 1600. A further descent by two lead miners is documented in 1760. The impressive wide shaft is 60m deep, and at its foot a low crawl leads into the large Main Chamber with a boulder slope floor. A climb of 24m up the east wall leads upwards into chambers with fine stalactites and flowstone, Millers Chamber and Damocles Rift.

Lloyd's description of 1770 noted a second shaft in the floor of the Main Chamber, leading to a stream cave at the bottom. This has never been seen in modern times but a dye test has shown that the limited drainage goes to the Main Rising in Speedwell Cavern. Lloyd made a rough survey (now one of the earliest known cave surveys), which is probably why his visit became so well known.

Once on the plateau you will join the "Limestone Way" **10**, a long-distance walking/cycling trail that goes from Matlock to Castleton – right across the White Peak *see p.61*. Follow the signs for Castleton and Cave Dale. Parts of the descent into Castleton village are rocky and slippery and extreme caution is required. For those who do not wish to attempt the descent a bridleway can be followed north past Rowter Farm to the road and thence back to Blue John Cavern.

As you start to descend into Cave Dale, the now famous Titan Shaft (the deepest in Britain) lies beneath Hurd Low to the left of the track and on private land (see map and front cover photograph). Cave Dale itself **11** is a fine limestone feature – a smaller version of the Winnats Pass. Like the Winnats Pass, this dry valley cuts through the reef belt but extends much further into the lagoonal limestones to the south. It probably originated by superimposition from the former shale cover and was enlarged by meltwater run-off and erosion when the ground remained frozen under periglacial conditions. About 700m from the bottom of the dale there are exposures of basaltic lava showing a crudely hexagonal columnar form. In the lower part of the dale there are a number of cavities that were enlarged by lead miners. The dale then narrows markedly before emerging into Castleton village.

12 CASTLETON VILLAGE

Castleton, which takes its name from Peveril Castle situated high on a reef limestone mass immediately to the south, is one of the most compact tourist attractions in the White Peak, with hotels, cafés and a Park Visitor Centre. The sale of Blue John ornaments is a particular speciality of the area.

Drainage of the Castleton valley is by the Peakshole Water, which flows eastwards to join the River Noe at Hope. This joins the River Derwent at Bamford, and eventually the Trent south of Derby. The Peakshole Water comes partly from two springs, Russet Well and Slop Moll, on either side of Peak Cavern gorge, and partly from a smaller stream flowing out of Peak Cavern itself. It is augmented by Odin Sitch, which drains the Millstone Grit upland of the Mam Tor–Losehill ridge to the north.

To the south and west of Castleton the steep north-facing limestone hillsides are the outer slopes of a complex of marginal reef limestones, similar in nature but much smaller than the outer edge of Australia's Great Barrier Reef. A massif of lagoonal limestones lies immediately to the south of the reef belt. The latter is broken by two dry valleys, Winnats Pass and Cave Dale: the heads of these are in the lagoonal limestones and they provide sections through the reef and fore-reef limestones.

Uplift soon after limestone sedimentation finished gave rise to erosion of the reef crest with resultant boulder beds and submarine screes low on the hillside near Treak Cliff Cavern, around Odin Mine and at Windy Knoll. The thick lenticular limestone reefs (also known as mud-mounds) with their steep outward dips are clearly visible in the higher cliffs of the Winnats Pass, in Cave Dale and in the sides of Peak Cavern gorge. Following uplift and erosion, there was renewed subsidence yielding a basin for reception of the deltaic sediments of the Millstone Grit Group.

In common with Buxton, Castleton has a cave that featured in the seven "Wonders of the Peak" described by Thomas Hobbs in 1678 and by Charles Cotton in 1681 – Peak Cavern, or "the Devil's Arse in the Peak". This is the largest and most impressive of the show caves in the area, if not in Britain!

Figure 17: **Peak Cavern,** looking out of the huge entrance where ropes used to be made
photo: Paul Deakin

13 PEAK CAVERN

Peak Cavern has the largest natural cave entrance in Britain, which lies beneath Peveril Castle at the head of a short blind gorge. The resurgence of the Peak Cavern stream lies just outside the entrance beneath the eastern cliff. Two other resurgences, Russet Well and Slop Moll, which discharge water from Speedwell Cavern, lie on either side of the Peak Cavern stream about 50m downstream of the resurgence.

The entrance chamber to Peak Cavern, the Vestibule, was once the site of a rope-walk, where rope was made by hand. This tradition was revived in the 1990s and rope making demonstrations are a feature of the cave tour. The rope-makers had cottages inside the Vestibule and the cavern roof is still partly blackened by soot from their chimney smoke. Avens in the roof have massive speleothems.

After the Vestibule, the cave soon closes down to Lumbago Walk and the Inner

Styx Passage. These are liable to flood to the roof in very wet weather. Beyond, the passage opens up again into the Great Cave, where features in the roof indicate upward dissolution when it was in the phreatic zone. Sediment slopes rise on both sides and have yielded animal bones from a fissure, now choked, in the floor of Cave Dale. An easy walk leads into Roger Rain's House, with its shower falling from a mineral vein rising into Cave Dale where a streamlet sinks. The tourist route ends at the top of the old "Devil's Staircase" which descends to meet the stream at the Halfway House.

From here a series of mudbanks lie along the flanks of a large phreatic tube with dissolutionally-enlarged joints above, making the Five Arches. The stream rises from Buxton Water Sump, dived for a distance of over 100m in 1949. Some 30m before the sump there is a junction where a small stream comes in from the right, and Victoria Aven, a large vein cavity, rises 90m to a series of joint passages and parallel avens. At stream level a low passage leads ahead into the Inferior Gallery, with such delights as the Mucky Ducks preceding a phreatic tube with limited vadose trenching. A branch on the right leads to The Treasury with a sump in the floor linking through to the Speedwell Cavern streamway, and a long crawl to the Rift Cavern higher up the streamway.

The Inferior Gallery continues to

Surprise View where there is a 6m drop into the Main Stream Passage. Downstream leads to the upstream end of Buxton Water Sump, whilst upstream a classic narrow canyon up to 20m high continues for another kilometre to Far Sump. A major branch on the south admits a tributary stream from Lake Passage, water coming from a deep phreatic zone beneath Dirtlow Rake. Another tributary comes from Main Stream Inlet above Squaws' Junction.

Far Sump is over 300m long and leads to Far Sump Extension, which terminate in two more sumps, but with an exciting series of dissolutionally-enlarged vein cavities above Stemple Highway. The old lead miners had found their way into Far Sump Extension from a passage in the roof of the Speedwell Cavern streamway and from the 80m-high Leviathan Cavern, whose top had been penetrated by lead miners at James Hall's Engine Mine (JH Mine) in the 18th century. Off to one side of Far Sump Extension a climb through large boulders leads to the bottom of Titan, a vein cavity 180m high, recently linked to the surface on Hurd Low, near upper Cave Dale, by an excavated shaft. The bottom 34m are largely boulder filled but the shaft is open for 146m (479ft) making it the highest vertical feature in any British cave system.

Avens rising from a branch passage near the Treasury lead to an extensive series of high-level passages some 40m above the stream caves. The profuse decoration with white speleothems has given them the name of the White River Series. Pits in the floor include the Moose Trap and a never-completed miners' link to Speedwell. A crawl leads to the top of Block Hall in Speedwell.

Peak Cavern's streamway is the largest and longest in the Peak District but its stream is a misfit, mostly derived from percolation water. In times of flood, when Speedwell's lower passage cannot cope with the flow, water rises and spills into Peak Cavern at several points, notably via the Treasury Sump.

Peak Cavern and its stream are graded to the present floor of Hope Valley but when it was an active resurgence much of the cave was in the phreatic zone. Earlier the Peak Cavern gorge may have been cut by water welling up from the cave mouth to spill onto a valley floor, which would then have been at a higher elevation.

Leave the village via the main road going west, which soon forks, with roads to Speedwell Cavern and the Winnats Pass to the left and to Treak Cliff Caverns and the landslide to the right. It is worth a visit to Speedwell Cavern at the entrance to the Winnats Pass before going on towards the landslide.

14 SPEEDWELL CAVERN

This is quite different from any other British show cave, for here the visitor traverses a partly flooded mine level driven almost due south in the 1770s to intersect west–east mineral veins at depth. You will be taken by boat along the Main Canal, some 500m in

Figure 18: The Inlet, Bung Hole Passage, Speedwell   *photo: Jerry Wooldridge*

length, as far as a large natural vein cavity known as the Bottomless Pit. One third of the way along the Main Canal is the inappropriately named Halfway House branch, which leads into vein cavity caverns extending beneath the Winnats Pass.

At the Bottomless Pit overflow water from the canals drops 15m into a lake 10m across with no visible way out. This water is next seen at Russet Well and Slop Moll. The Far Canal continues some 300m beyond the Pit before bending to a westerly course close to New Rake. Soon after the bend an inactive tributary passage was intersected by the Far Canal. On the right (north) the crawl leads to a low tortuous passage rightly called the Assault Course by the first explorers. It passes under the foot of a series of descents and crawls entered from a mine shaft on the surface, and described by Pilkington in 1789.

After a further 150m the Far Canal tunnel intersects a major stream cave system draining from west to east close to New Rake. A short distance upstream at the Pit Props a branch off to the left leads into old lead miners' stopes. Continuing upstream, Whirlpool Passage is a major tributary that meets the main streamway at the deep Whirlpool, where swimming was necessary until a fixed traverse line was installed. The tributary comes from the Whirlpool Rising, which ebbs and flows at intervals of a few minutes at certain states of flow, indicating a complex series of syphons upstream.

After passing the Whirlpool a natural cave passage leads upstream to the Boulder Piles where there has been a collapse from mine workings above. A by-pass was found and digging provided a route into the base of the Leviathan vein cavity. The top of this high cavern was also reached by lead miners from JH Mine on the surface far above. A low passage links the foot of Leviathan with Stemple Highway in Far Sump Extension

see description of Peak Cavern, page 29.

At the upstream end of the Speedwell streamway is the Main Rising, a complex sump that has been explored by cave divers for more than 250m to a point where it continues but at a depth of 72m. A few metres downstream of the Rising, on the south side, is Cliff Passage from which a small stream enters. A now famous piece of graffiti, the Miners' Toast scratched on the mud-coated wall reads "A Health to All Miners and Mentainers of Mines, October 20th 1781 J.I.B. M.N." Beyond this inscription Cliff Passage leads to the bottom of the 50m-high Cliff Cavern which has been climbed to enter two rift passages, Cliffhanger and Joint Effort. Two small streams enter these rifts from impenetrable sumps and the water cascades down Cliff Cavern.

On the opposite wall to Cliff Passage and a few tens of metres downstream a 5m climb leads to the short Bathing Pool passage. At its end a large pool 16m deep occupies the whole chamber and there is no way on. The nearby Secret Sump has been dived to a depth of about -40m but appears not to be connected.

Returning to the junction of the Far Canal and the streamway, a short heading on the south leads to the Bung Hole Series, a 600m-long downstream continuation of the streamway. The Bung Hole takes its name from a dam some 6m high built to maintain boating depth water in the canals. Downstream of this dam, the canyon cutting phase has not proceeded so far and the stream flows over a long series of cascades and potholes before disappearing where water meets roof at the same level as Russet Well and Slop Moll. Shortly beyond the dam a large cavern on the right is Block Hall, a major vein cavity at the top of which a low crawl connects with the White River Series, first entered from Peak Cavern. Partway down the Bung Hole watercourse is Rift

Cavern with Egnaro Aven rising to Colostomy Crawl, also linking Speedwell with Peak Cavern.

With sumps at both ends, the Speedwell Cavern stream cave forms the main underground drainage route of the Castleton area. The sectors between the swallets and Main Rising and between the downstream terminal sump and Russet Well are totally submerged and unlikely ever to be fully explored. Movement of the water through these sectors is largely along mineral veins and penetrates to depths greater than 70m along extended U-tube systems. It is likely that part of the route is through vein cavities which are continuing to be enlarged by the aggressive water.

From Speedwell there are two routes back to your starting point. Either the steep but technically easy ride up Winnats Pass, or the more gradual and interesting ride up what remains of the eastern leg of the former A625 past Treak Cliff Cavern to the great

Figure 19: Treak Cliff Cavern *photo: T D Ford*

landslide beneath Mam Tor. Irrespective of the choice of route, walk about 100 metres up the Winnats Pass from the Speedwell Cavern car park to see the entrance to Suicide Cave. This is of importance because it is believed to pre-date downcutting of the gorge to its present level. Sediments in the cave exhibit a close similarity to those in Treak Cliff Cavern and it seems likely that the two caves were once part of the same drainage system.

15 WINNATS PASS

There has been considerable speculation over the origin of this spectacular relict gorge that is over 130 metres deep and cuts through the belt of marginal reef limestones. The favoured explanation is that the Pass was initially a shallow channel cut through the reef belt in mid-Carboniferous times but later filled with shales of the Millstone Grit Group. It was probably re-excavated by meltwater running off a snow-and-ice field near the present Windy Knoll area in the later parts of the Pleistocene. No evidence has been found to support popular stories that it was formed by cavern collapse.

16 TREAK CLIFF CAVERN

From Speedwell ride back down the hill and turn left at the road junction, signposted Treak Cliff Cavern and "cul-de-sac". After about 500m a well-marked path on the left leads up to the cavern.

Located on the east face of the steep fore-reef slope of Treak Cliff, the first part of this cave was discovered by miners in the 18th century. It was extended into the stalactite caverns by fluorspar miners in 1926. The present entrance uses the original mine tunnel which has exposures of basal Millstone Grit Group shales in its walls. Scattered limestone boulders enclosed within the shale are part of the Boulder Bed, evidence for a mid-Carboniferous phase of uplift and erosion of the reef crest.

The now famous Blue John fluorspar was deposited in the voids between the limestone boulders and in fissures in the underlying limestones. The first section of the cavern has been modified by miners extracting Blue John, but evidence of it having been a phreatic cave system dissolved out of the mid-Carboniferous Boulder Bed is widespread. Palaeokarstic cavities and pipe-veins lined with Blue John are present within the reef limestones.

The second section of Treak Cliff Cavern is a sharp contrast in that its chambers are parts of a vadose canyon without modification by miners. Passages in the roof lead up to a former entrance on the hillside that has now been blocked to prevent unauthorised access. This entrance was a former swallet for a stream that drained a former, much larger, extent of the Millstone Grit uplands. A meandering phreatic tube can be seen in the roof, but the vadose canyon floor is concealed by fallen blocks.

The tourist route and the canyon end at a massive collapsed boulder which has not been passed by cavers. The most striking features of Treak Cliff Cavern are the Blue John veins in the first section and the abundant stalactites, stalagmites, flowstone and helictites in the second section. Some stalagmites in the Dream Cave have grown on a floor of inwashed loessic mud. Treak Cliff Cavern is an abandoned, relict, cave and the former outfall of its drainage is unknown although similarities in sediment deposits suggest that it was once linked to Suicide Cave. The Cavern receives abundant percolation water and dye tracing has shown that this now drains to Russet Well and Slop Moll.

After your visit to Treak Cliff Cavern continue up the old road which is well surfaced as far as a turning circle at the foot of

Figure 20: Mam Tor landslip photo: Tony Waltham

the Mam Tor landslide. A short distance before this on the right are the remains of the Odin mine waste heaps with a fine crushing circle and wheel, whilst on the left is Odin Gorge and the entrance to Odin Cave. This is a short (42m) abandoned remnant of what was once a more extensive phreatic cave formed on the junction of the Treak Cliff Boulder Bed and the underlying limestone.

17 THE MAM TOR LANDSLIP

Between the vehicular access to Blue John Cavern (via minor roads from the west the most northerly of which was formerly the A625) and the vehicular access to Treak Cliff Cavern (via the A6187 (formerly the A625) from Castleton) there is a remarkable landscape feature, the Mam Tor Landslip. Up until 1976 the A625 had been a major trunk road crossing of the Pennines and was one of the lowest and easiest crossings between Greater Manchester and the Sheffield area, especially in times of snowfall. Prior to this there had periodically been cracks in the road and they had been patched up, but then quite suddenly in late 1975 there was a major slippage of the road bed.

Although it is now thought that the earth movement here has been going on for over 4,000 years, it seems extremely providential that the road, built about 1800, sur-

Figure 21: Detail of the Mam Tor landslip. Engineering efforts to retain this portion of the A625 Manchester-Sheffield trunk road ceased in 1976 after a major landslip. It is now an 'interesting' footpath, or in parts a challenging cycle ride! *photo: Tony Waltham*

vived for as long as it did. As with many landslides, ingress of water lubricates internal slip surfaces and enhances the process. Thus in wetter seasons the movement tends to speed up and in drier ones it slows down. Studies since 1979 have shown that there is over 3.2Mm³ of slipped material and that the area affected is over 1km long with a fall of 270m beneath a 70m-high head scar.

Cyclists - take care in crossing this feature on your way back to the Blue John Cavern car park as there are chunks of old road-bed all over the place, with sizeable steps between some of them.

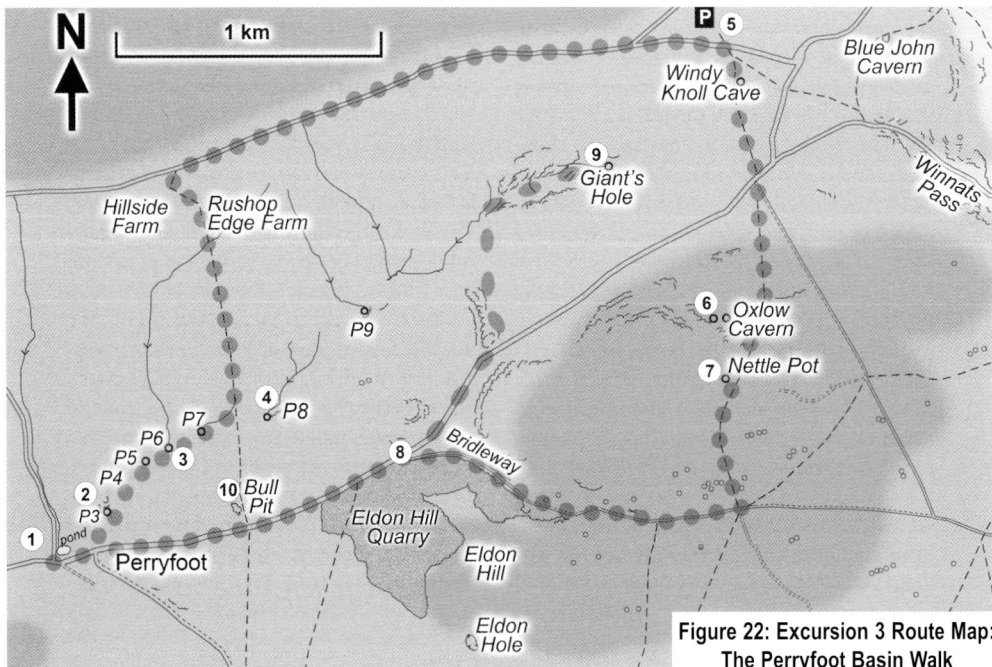

Figure 22: Excursion 3 Route Map: The Perryfoot Basin Walk

EXCURSION 3: THE PERRYFOOT BASIN WALK 8-10km

A walk around the Perryfoot drainage basin, where part of the waters of the Castleton caves originate and disappear below ground. An area where natural caves, and cavities created by the lead miners of the 19th century and before, are closely intertwined.

Recommended start point, at the side of, or near to the the minor road close to Perryfoot Farm **1**.

See Excursion 2, for discussion of the geology and hydrology of this area.

The first section of this route (from **1** to **4**) is not a public right of way. You should first call at Perryfoot Farm, ask permission and pay the "trespass fee".

You first pass P2, Sheepwash Swallet, the most westerly of the stream-sinks to have been traced to P8 cave. The lead miners seem to have been aware of this as they diverted water from the P1 sink (which flows into Coalpithole Mine) to P2. Not far beyond, a large tree-lined depression marks the entrance to Gautries Hole **2**, where a small stream from a field drain sinks. Just inside the cave entrance a larger stream is met and the combined flow has been traced to P8. The cave contains some 240m of muddy passage and streamway. You next pass the P4 and P5 swallets, closely followed by P6 and the collapse doline known as Little Bull Pit **3** that is adjacent to it. The stream that sinks here is larger than that at P8 but it has washed so much sediment into the swallet that it has defeated all attempts to gain access to further cave passages. In common with P2 to P5, the water sinking at P6 is next seen when it emerges from a sump in P8. This is also the case with the next sink – known (not surprisingly) as P7.

After passing P7 the private footpath crosses a Public Footpath that links directly from the main road to the right. If you continue straight ahead on the private footpath you will reach P8, the second longest of the Castleton swallet caves with over 1500m of passage. The stream that sinks at the entrance can be followed down two vertical cascades (8m and 6m) before sinking in the floor. A second stream emerges from a sump and can be followed downstream to yet another sump. Diving has revealed a series of sumps beyond this with intervening stream passage. Permission to visit P8 and the other nearby swallets should be obtained from Perryfoot Farm.

Return to the Public Footpath, turn right and head uphill (to the north) towards Rushop Edge Farm. When you reach the road (formerly the A625) turn right and follow this for 2.3km until you see the next Public Footpath sign on the right **5**. (Note that just before this footpath there is a large car park on your left at the base of Mam Tor, which is an alternative starting point for this circular walk). From the road there are good views across Rushup Vale and the stream-sinks that mark the northernmost edge of the limestone outcrop to the abandoned limestone quarry that has eaten into the side of Eldon Hill.

From **5** the footpath heads south to a minor road, but after only a few metres you will pass Windy Knoll Cave on your right. Part of the entrance collapsed in 2005 and is now fenced off for safety. This is an ancient, relict cave uncovered by 19th century quarrying. The eroded crest of the reef is covered by boulder beds that form the cave roof. Neptunean dykes filled with boulders and shale are visible in the old quarry face.

35

Bituminous hydrocarbons, collectively known as elaterite, are the last relics of an ancient oilfield; the bitumens ooze out of the limestone and the boulder bed.

Cross the road and on the opposite side follow the footpath up the low hillside where you will soon pass a 20m-deep mine shaft that is the entrance to Oxlow Cavern **6**. The mine shaft leads to a series of large vertical mineral vein cavities, formed by an early phase of phreatic dissolution along the weakness provided by the west–east Faucet Rake. About 200m to the west an alternative entrance is provided by the nearly vertical Maskhill Mine shaft and caverns. If the link passage through to the lower end of Giants Hole is included there is a system here that is over 200m deep, one of the deepest in England.

Shallow channels have been cut into the loess sheet around here and they drain into blocked fissures in a mineral vein. The former outcrops of the mineral veins are clearly shown by lines of hollows once containing shafts and surrounded by low hillocks of waste from the mines. A dozen or so veins can be traced across the moor. They lie along the projected trend of the subterranean drainage from Perryfoot to Castleton, though the active water-course lies at least 200m below ground.

Much of this moor between Eldon Hill and Castleton has a subsoil of yellowish silty clay, a metre or so in thickness. Seen only in temporary excavations and pits from which fluorite has been excavated this is weathered loess, a wind-blown dust, which was derived from adjacent areas that had been scoured by the earlier Pleistocene glaciers or which had been laid bare during the tundra conditions of the late Pleistocene. Much of the glutinous mud for which Peak District caves are notorious is derived from part of this loessic clay that has been washed down fissures.

In the next pasture you will pass close to Nettle Pot **7**. There is not much to see on the surface here, but this deep narrow pot was opened by digging in the 1930s and is a vertical cave system, unusual in Derbyshire. The entrance shaft is 49m deep to The Flats, a series of bedding passages and small rifts developed along a thick clay-wayboard (an altered volcanic tuff). Below this are three joint-oriented pots, Elizabeth, Beza and Crumble, each of which is more than 50m deep. Narrow crawls lead to a sump at the bottom.

Permission from Oxlow Farm is required to visit the Oxlow Caverns, Maskhill Mine and Nettle Pot locations.

Continue over the low hill until you come to a stile at a six-ways junction. Here turn hard right and follow the Public Bridleway back to the road **8**. You will descend close to the end of the main face of the now abandoned Eldon Hill Quarry. Unlike some Derbyshire limestone quarries this one is in a very prominent situation and during its working life the quarry cut into several caves. Only

Figure 23: Oxlow Cavern, East Chamber
photo: Jerry Wooldridge

Figure 24: Entrance to Giants Hole *photo: Tony Waltham*

stalactite-decorated avens can be seen above. Ancient passages completely choked with sandy gravel can be seen in the walls near these avens. Below the 6m-high Garlands Pot waterfall the stream flows in a high, narrow and meandering vadose canyon ("the Crabwalk") for over 600m. The Crabwalk is followed by the somewhat wider "Great Relief Passage" which ends at a sump. This can be by-passed via the Eating House and the stream is met again close to the bottom of Geology Pot. Downstream the passage can be followed to the East Canal which is 128m below the cave entrance. A sump in East Canal has been dived for 137m and to a depth of 30m. In addition to the active passages there is a network of largely relict passages including a link to Oxlow Caverns.

Return up the private road to the main road and follow it past the Bridleway towards Perryfoot. After 600m you will see a Public Footpath on your right and this runs past Bull Pit **10** to the P7 swallet that you passed at the start of the walk. Bull Pit is a 25m-deep steep-sided collapse doline. Attempts to gain access into the cavern into which the collapse presumably occurred have so far failed.

It is now about 800m back to your start point near Perryfoot Farm, but just a few metres further along the road towards Sparrowpit look over the wall on your right. Two swallet caves open from the same depression – Perryfoot Cave and Dr Jackson's Cave. These, and their relationship to the drainage, are described as stop 3 on Cycle Ride 2.

two open caves remain, Sidetrack Cave, a short high-level segment of a stream cave in the eastern wall, and Alsop's Cave, which was partly destroyed by quarrying. In addition to the open cave passage there are a series of very old phreatic tubes and vadose canyons in the west-central wall, but these are entirely filled with sands and clays probably derived from Rushup Edge long before the Rushup Vale had been eroded to its present depth. An isolated buttress near the quarry entrance is coated with weathered speleothems.

You will soon join the main road and turning left will take you back to Perryfoot. However, if you turn right and follow the road for some 600m there is a private road on your left leading to Peakshill Farm and Giants Hole **9**. If you wish to visit the entrance to Giant's Hole you need to first visit the farm and pay a trespass fee. The entrance to Giants Hole is swallet P12 and the stream that sinks here has formed the most extensive of the Rushup Vale swallet caves with over 4km of passage. The first 300m was enlarged by blasting in the 1960s when there were plans to open the cave to the public that never came to fruition. What was once quite arduous caving is now easy walking in the streamway and impressive

37

EXCURSION 4:
THE EYAM and STONEY MIDDLETON AREA

Centred upon the villages of Eyam and Stoney Middleton lies a compact and complex area of cave development. Although located on the northeastern limit of the limestone outcrop, this area has the second largest number and length of caves in the White Peak. Streams with their origins to the north, on the prominent Millstone Grit Group escarpment of Eyam Edge, flow south across the shales and sink close to the first contact with the limestone beds. Unfortunately the A623 trunk road runs all the way down Middleton Dale, on its descent from the limestone plateau to the Derwent Valley at Calver. This is a busy highway, made all the more so by the closure of the A625 some years ago *see the Mam Tor landslip p.33*. Also, the few public rights of way in the area do not, in the main, pass close to the features of interest, so it is not possible to suggest a sensible circular walk or cycle ride. We therefore simply list the features of interest and locate them by their numbers on the key map.

DIVERGENT DRAINAGE

One of the interesting features of this area is its divergent drainage. Sinking streams have been shown by water tracing to emerge at points several kilometres apart. For example, sinks to the west, such as Mrs Smyth's Swallet, drain northwest to the Bagshawe Resurgence, southeast to Watergrove Sough, and eastsoutheast to Moorwood Sough **15**.

Farther east, Waterfall Swallet **1** drains to Watergrove **9**, Moorwood and Stoke Soughs. Prior to the driving of these mine drainage levels (soughs) is seems likely that the two dominant natural springs were the Bagshawe Resurgence in Bradwell and the Carlswark Resurgence **12** in Stoney Middleton. However, there are other smaller springs such as the Ooms in Bradwell and the thermal spring in Stoney Middleton, both of which discharge some water from the sinks.

An additional complexity is that water tracing suggests that a small amount from the sinks targets an estavelle (a sink that can sometimes be a rising) at Wardlow Mires near the head of Cressbrook Dale. Water also runs off a small Millstone Grit Group outlier centred on Wardlow Mires.

In the caves, dry upper levels indicate a progressive evolution as the local base level in Middleton Dale fell. Many of the passages can be related to specific horizons within the limestone sequence, including two Shell Beds packed with fossil "Gigantoproductid" shells.

1 WATERFALL SWALLET

This large, tree-lined depression is situated 800m east of Foolow, close to the edge of the limestone outcrop. It is developed on a mineralized fault, Crosslow Vein, and has formed by collapse into dissolutionally enlarged cavities. A stream that cascades down the northwest side and gives the site its name normally sinks at three points in the floor. However, after heavy rainfall water backs up flooding the depression to a depth of several metres before escaping into the bedding plane entrance to Waterfall Hole in the northern cliff. This is a complex 43m-deep three-dimensional maze of collapsed and eroded blocks in narrow rifts and bedding plane passages.

Crack Pot can be found in the same depression. It contains extensive deposits of orange clay.

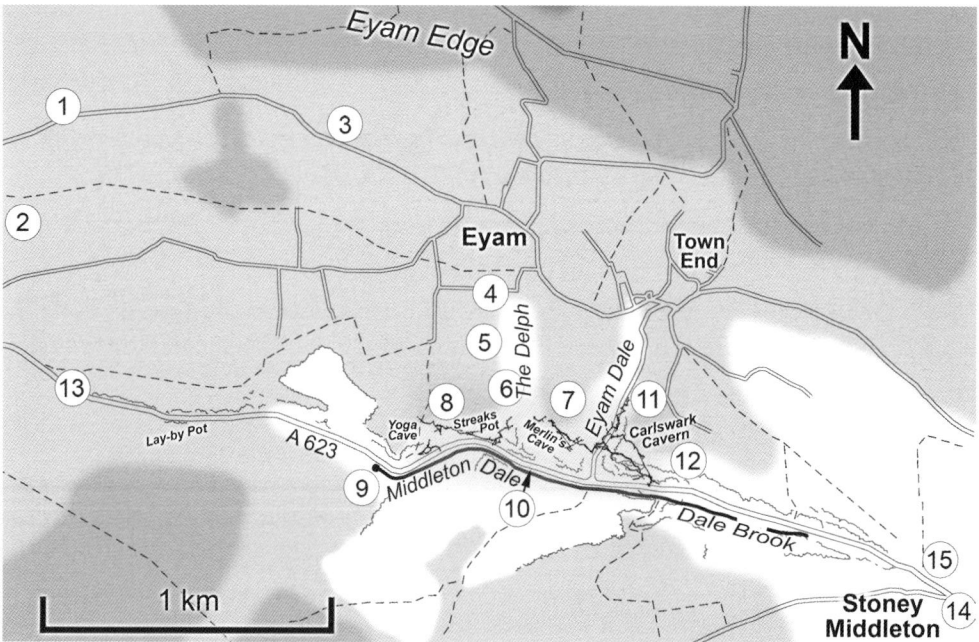

Figure 25: Excursion 4 Location Map: The Eyam and Stoney Middleton Area.

2 LINEN DALE

The dale commences as a shallow dry valley a few metres south of Waterfall Swallet. It is a tributary of the more deeply incised dry gorge of Middleton Dale and was progressively desiccated by loss of surface drainage as the underground system developed. A small (14m) cave in a small disused quarry at the northern end of the valley was probably a former swallet.

3 HUNGERHILL SWALLET

Hungerhill Swallet is a medium sized doline on the shale/limestone margin. The cave was discovered by excavation in 1987 and has been explored to a depth of 76m, including a spectacular 40m pitch, "Deep Space". The stream sinks a little further to the west and is met underground. The cave is formed on the same vein system as Waterfall Swallet, but does not show the same degree of breakdown. It contains very large joint-controlled cavities, some of which are well decorated with unusual speleothems.

4 THE SALTPAN

This curiously-named feature is a narrow limestone gorge, 5 to 10m deep, at the head of Cucklet Delph ("The Delph"). A small stream, Jumber Brook, rises from a culvert at the head of the gorge but the present day stream is a misfit too small to have cut the valley. Instead the Saltpan is thought to have been a swallet cave when the shale margin lay farther to the south and subsequently to have been unroofed and modified by surface processes.

5 CUCKLET CHURCH CAVE

All that remains of this ancient cave system is a series of interconnected arches in a prominent buttress high on the west side of the Delph. The name stems from use of the site for religious purposes during the Great Plague of 1665, and a Plague Commemoration Service is still held here each year.

6 CUCKLET DELPH SWALLETS

Jumber Brook loses water at two distinct

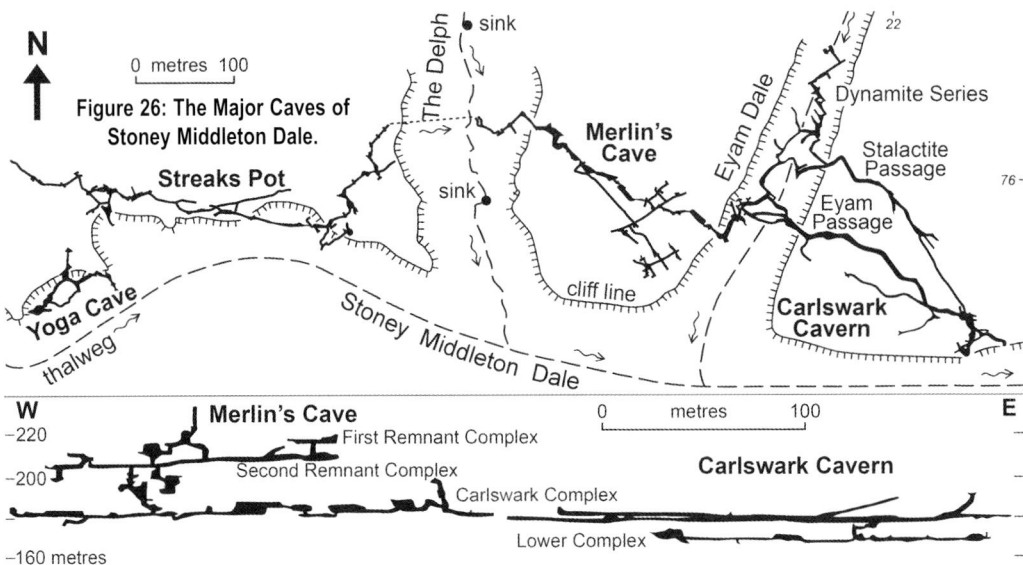

Figure 26: The Major Caves of Stoney Middleton Dale.

points on its journey towards Middleton Dale, the Upper Swallet which has been dye-traced direct to Moorwood Sough, and the Lower Swallet which drains into the Merlin Streamway of Carlswark Cavern. Both have been dug, the upper to a depth of over 10m, but no penetrable passage has been discovered.

7 DELPH HOLE

High on the east side of Cucklet Delph, this short mine level gives access to ancient sediment-filled phreatic passages; total length 50m. Almost opposite on the west side is Nicker Grove Mine through which access has been gained to natural cave passage in Streaks Pot.

8 STREAKS POT and YOGA CAVE

Both caves have small entrances a few metres above the road on the north side of Middleton Dale. Yoga Cave contains 185m of relict and largely horizontal passages, mainly developed at the base of the Lower Shell Bed. Streaks Pot has 770m of passage with an upper entrance 45m above the dale floor. The lower series is active and carries a large stream in wet weather.

9 WATERGROVE SOUGH TAIL

The Sough was driven to dewater Watergrove Mine farther to the west, but has also captured a significant proportion of the natural underground drainage. Upstream from the sough tail Middleton Dale is perennially dry and contains only one cave system of any size, Lay-by Pot, which is 370m long and 23m deep. The nearby Furness Quarry has a short sediment-choked cave high in the east wall.

10 HAWKENEDGE WELL

The well discharges a consistent flow of water from an unknown catchment south of the dale. The site is also referred to as Oakenedge Sough but it is by no means certain whether the present flow of water is from a natural spring or from a sough.

11 EYAM DALE

This short, steep gorge on the north side of Middleton Dale has a small, largely culverted misfit stream, Hollow Brook, which has probably only occupied the valley since the blockage of swallets to the north of Eyam village. On the west side of Eyam Dale, opposite the electricity sub-station, are two entrances to Merlin's Mine/Cavern, a com-

13-14   MIDDLETON DALE

The dale is a 3km-long gorge incised along the strike of the limestones on the northern flank of an anticline. It has had a complicated geomorpho-logical history, with early valley development masked by later glacia-tion, as shown by deposits of till on the much quarried south flank. Postglacial incision was probably under periglacial, frozen ground conditions, and only a misfit stream flowing from Watergrove Sough, with tributary inputs from Jumber Brook, Hollow Brook and Hawkenedge Well occupies the Dale today.

15   MOORWOOD SOUGH TAIL

The Sough was driven to de-water mines between Stoney Middleton, Eyam and Wardlow and it has captured water from a wide area. Its tail lies in the private grounds of Stoney Middleton Hall. It is the artificial resurgence for the Carlswark and Merlin stream.

plex of mined levels and natural passages. Digging at the bottom of one shaft gave access to the Merlin's Streamway and upstream there are eight sumps with large open streamway between them. Downstream a flooded passage connects with Carlswark Cavern. Access to Carlswark was also gained via a well decorated pas-sage, Gimli's Dream, but the connection was blocked after substantial vandalism.

12   CARLSWARK CAVERN

Combined with Merlin's Cavern the Carlswark Complex has some 3.2km of pas-sages. These lie beneath the northern cliffs of Middleton Dale and extend westwards under Eyam Dale almost to the Delph. The original entrance was an arch close to road level, but that most used today is on the Gin terrace on the north side of the Dale. Here a short mine level leads into the relict Eyam Passage, a typical phreatic tube with vadose trench, long abandoned by the stream. The Shell Bed with its silicified "Gigantoproductid" shells crowded together is well exposed in the roof. Stalagmite bosses and plen-ty of muddy sediments constrict the passage, which extends into the parallel Stalactite Passage leading to the down-stream sector of a long sump. Upstream an excavated passage leads to the active Merlin Streamway.

Figure 28: Carlswark Cavern, false floor photo: J Wooldridge

41

EXCURSION 5: THE WYE VALLEY

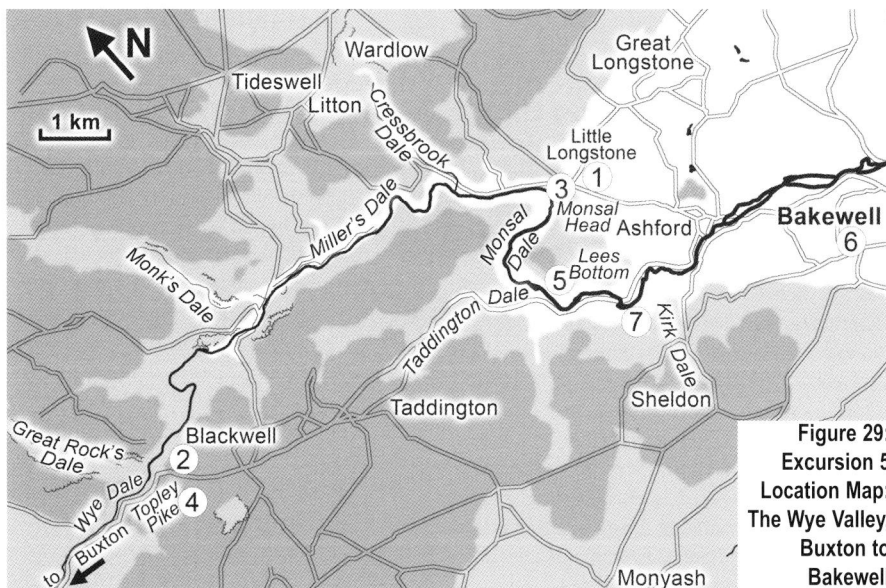

Figure 29:
Excursion 5
Location Map:
The Wye Valley,
Buxton to
Bakewell

The River Wye is the only major river to cross the White Peak. Its course from near Buxton to Bakewell is around 25km long and is incised into the limestone plateau by nearly 200m in its middle section. It is the finest example of an allogenic valley in the White Peak, with extensive cliffs that provide challenging rock-climbs interspersed with sections of scree. In addition the river is augmented by many springs that enter via brooks or directly into its bed. These are particularly noticeable in times of drought when the flow at Ashford may be up to ten times that at Buxton. These springs drain a large but poorly defined catchment that extends north and south of the river. To the north this almost certainly extends to Dove Holes, but two stream sinks in the village have been captured by a railway tunnel and now discharge into the Irish Sea via the Goyt and Mersey.

The Wye Valley has several separately named sections. Leaving Buxton as Ashwood Dale, it soon becomes Wye Dale, then Chee Dale, followed by Miller's Dale, Water-cum-Jolly Dale, Monsal Dale and Ashford Dale. From the mouth of the currently sealed tunnel beneath Monsal Head the, "Monsal Trail" follows most of the line of the former LMS Railway from Bakewell up to Buxton. This was a fine piece of Victorian engineering, with its numerous tunnels, bridges and viaducts. From Bakewell almost to Monsal Head this is now a joint walking/cycling trail but none of the finest sections that traverse the valley itself, from beneath Monsal Head to its abrupt termination some 5km short of Buxton are currently available to cyclists.

Much of the deep incision of the central section is due to glacial meltwater discharge, and terraces with relics of till occur around Monsal Dale and Bakewell. Lava sheets are present not far below the valley floor and may assist in maintaining surface flow. With its high limestone walls one might have expected many caves but they are few and short.

Monks Dale is a deep tributary valley occupied by a small intermittent stream that is partly fed by springs perched on a lava bed. Lumb Hole, has an obvious entrance about 500m up Cressbrook Dale and is also situated a few metres above a lava bed. There is little more than 20m of accessible cave passage but in wet weather it discharges a large stream. At the bottom of Taddington Dale are the six Lees Bottom springs two of which are actively depositing tufa. Further downstream and to the south of the A6 there are two natural springs in Great Shacklow Wood and beyond these is the tail of Magpie Sough **7**, *see Fig 8.* This lead-mine drainage level extends for some 1500m beneath the Sheldon area to the south as far as Magpie Mine. However, water tracing experiments have shown that it has captured drainage from a much wider area, The main input of water to the sough is from a "boil-up" on a mineral vein. The inactive Blende Vein is partly a phreatic cave developed along a pipe vein.

Although not offering much by way of caves, the Wye Valley is a fine feature of the White Peak, well worth exploring in part or in its entirety, by bicycle or on foot. Some of the more dramatic viewpoints are described below.

VIEWPOINTS
Reference numbers here are to those shown **1-7** on Figure 29, page 42.

1-2 THE MONSAL TRAIL
In its walking section from Wye Dale to Miller's Dale this provides some spectacular views, especially from the bridges and viaducts where the former railway line struggled to ascend the valley on its cross-country route to Manchester via its summit

at the head of Peak Dale, with its short branch line to Buxton.

3 MONSAL HEAD
Situated on the B6465 Wardlow to Ashford-in-the-Water road, Monsal Head is a very popular tourist site with a large hotel/pub, plenty of parking space, and well maintained public toilets. The reason for this focus of facilities is one of the most dramatic views in the White Peak. Looking up the Wye Valley there is Cressbrook, Cressbrook Hall and the tributary Cressbrook Dale which can be walked all the way to its diminutive start at Wardlow Mires. Looking down-valley there is the huge sweep southwards of Monsal Dale to its meeting with Taddington Dale and Deep Dale, with the old railway bridge revealing its dramatic scale

4 TOPLEY PIKE
The A6 follows the Wye Valley out of Buxton, first through Ashwood Dale and then Wye Dale, before making its steep ascent out of the valley and across higher ground to Taddington. At the bottom of this hill the entrance to Topley Pike Quarry is on the right and on the left there is a car-park **2** provided for, and close-by, the Monsal Trail. Near the top of the hill, on its final right hand sweep, there is another car park on the left side of the road. From here there is an excellent view up Wye Dale to the left, down Chee Dale to the right and up a major dry tributary, Great Rocks Dale, straight ahead. This is also a good vantage point from which to assess the extent of limestone quarrying across this part of the White Peak. The major working quarry, Tunstead, lies outside the National Park but, controversially, planning permission was granted for a major extension into the Park on the grounds of the very high purity of the stone and the fact that the quarry has a railhead, which substantially reduces the amount of product sent by road.

Whilst this is a positive feature the fact that this line, which continues to Topley Pike Quarry and on to Buxton, is still active as a mineral railway means that the Monsal Trail comes to its abrupt current end. The line up Great Rocks Dale past Tunstead and Dove Holes quarries is the former LMS main line to Manchester and continues through the 2.7km-long Dove Holes Tunnel to Chapel en le Frith. When the tunnel was driven springs were intersected and channelled to the Chapel end. As noted above, water tracing experiments have shown that two stream sinks in Dove Holes village discharge into the railway tunnel, and thence to the Goyt and Mersey.

5 LEES BOTTOM

Here there is another car park and picnic area at the side of the A6. The road has just descended the tributary Taddington Dale to rejoin the main Wye Valley. But it joins it at a dramatic spot as it is coming out of its deepest gorge section. Looking back upstream, on the right is Fin Cop (327m), the site of a Bronze Age settlement, and to the south the remains of another early settlement and a rock shelter have been found. Below here the valley gradually widens out and the river starts to meander across its broadening flood-plain.

6 BAKEWELL

Bakewell is the largest settlement within the Peak Park, a thriving market town and visitor centre, and Headquarters of the Peak District National Park Authority.

---- ---- ～～～ ---- ----

THE DOVE and MANIFOLD VALLEYS

The Dove and the Manifold rivers have extensive catchments on Millstone Grit Group sandstones and shales in their upper reaches before traversing the western margin of the limestone outcrop. Both meander through a belt of bedded limestones with scattered reefs. The Dove maintains a continuous flow across the limestone outcrop, partly ensured by puddled clay floors behind the numerous fishing weirs, but the Manifold is ephemeral in its middle reach.

Our area of interest here is principally those sections of the Dove, between Hartington and Ilam, and of its most important tributary, the Manifold, below Hulme End, where they carve almost parallel ravines through the limestone strata before eventually coming together between Ilam and Thorpe. By anybody's standards they are both exceptionally beautiful limestone valleys.

Downstream of Ilam the Dove leaves the White Peak and meanders southwards, to be joined by the Bradbourne Brook and the Henmore Brook (the Ashbourne river). It then continues its meandering course before eventually joining the Trent near Burton. It has left the high limestone plateau of its upper course to flow over Triassic sandstones and mudstones. These are less resistant to erosion than the limestones and as a result the scenery here is less dramatic and more rounded and undulating than that of the White Peak.

The DCA publication, *A Cave+Mine Conservation Audit for the Manifold & Hamps Valleys* (2005) contains a detailed record of known caves+abandoned mines in the area traversed by Excursions 6 and 7. Reference to this valuable publication is recomended for further information on the geology, hydrology, archaeology and biospeleology of this area. *See box on page 64.*

EXCURSION 6: CLASSIC DOVE and MANIFOLD WALK
Distance: 12km

The suggested starting point for this walk is in or near the hamlet of Stanshope **1**. In the high season parking may be difficult and the public car parks in Dovedale (below the Izaak Walton Hotel), or at the National Trust's Ilam Hall (free to its members) provide alternative starting points. Either way we suggest that you proceed in a clockwise direction.

Leave Stanshope by the lane going east, and then take the signed footpath right after a few metres. This soon starts to descend into Hall Dale **2**, a characteristically steep, deeply incised, tributary dry valley that has extensive scree deposits at its lower end. After a further kilometre you will join the main valley of Dove Dale in its most heavily wooded section. Follow it downstream for 400m to the footbridge **3**.

On crossing the river here, Ilam Rock and Pickering Tor dominate the landscape on opposite sides and each has its own

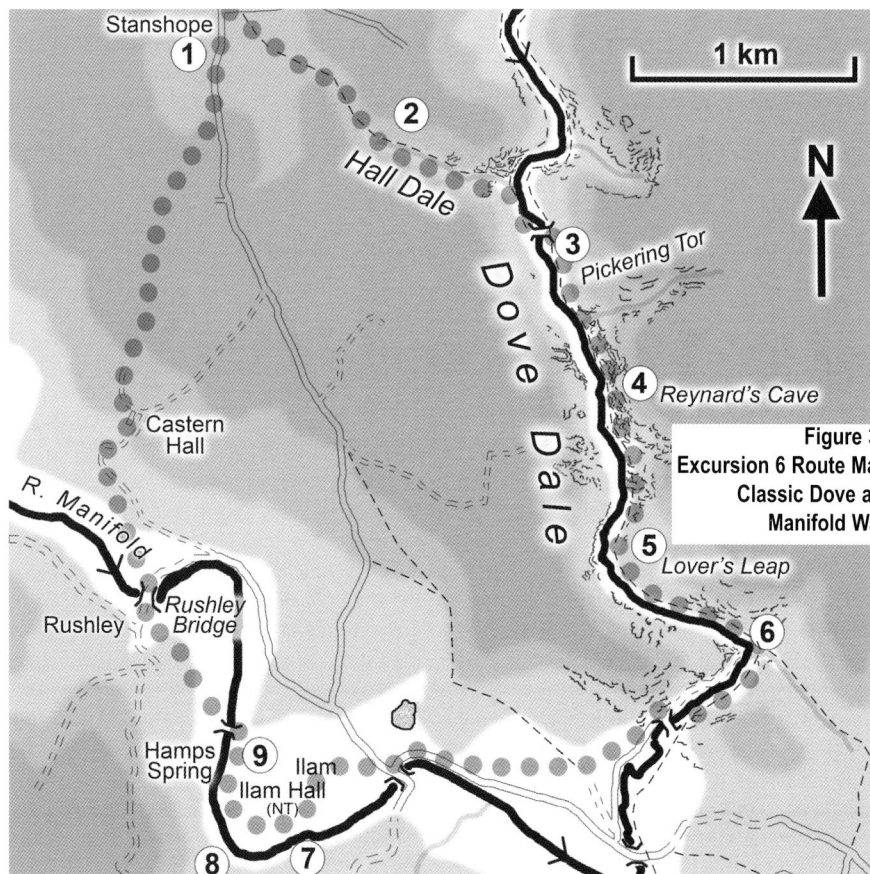

Figure 30:
Excursion 6 Route Map:
Classic Dove and
Manifold Walk

Figure 31: Ilam Rock, Dovedale   *photo: Tony Waltham*

Leap **5,** one of several so named features in the Peak District, associated with legends of fleeing lovers. There is a small resurgence cave at river level below Lover's Leap and on the opposite bank a few metres downstream are crags known as the Twelve Apostles.

The valley now takes an acute right turn and the famous Stepping Stones come into view **6**. You may cross here, or if you prefer it there is a footbridge a few metres further along. As the valley starts to open out before the confluence with the Manifold, take a footpath right that cuts across the shoulder of the hillside and behind the Izaak Walton Hotel. This leads through Ilam village, past the church and down to the Ilam Risings **7**. These are close to the National Trust's Ilam Hall where there is a Visitor Centre, Youth Hostel and car park.

Under drought conditions virtually the entire flow of the Manifold comes from six risings in close proximity but with different catchment areas. The lowest are Weir and Well risings which are thought to discharge only autogenic percolation water. Next are the Raspberry, Main and Ripple Risings which are in the River channel below Ilam Hall and are fed by the River Manifold sinks. Finally, the Upper Rising issues from a small, railed grotto to the north of the path and is fed by the River Hamps sink at Waterhouses. There does not appear to be any intermixing of Hamps and Manifold waters. The Main Rising has been penetrated by divers for about 267m, reaching a depth of 53.5m.

Follow the River upstream and soon you come to the Hinkley Wood Risings **8** in the right bank of the Manifold. Water tracing

caves. Although they are situated close together on opposite banks of the river, these caves appear to be genetically unrelated. Ilam Rock is a detached limestone tower within which the cave, a single chamber, contains tufaceous speleothems. Pickering Tor Cave is a small, relict phreatic cave.

Soon the impressive arch of Reynard's Cave **4**, comes into view. It stands some 30m above the valley floor and is 10m high. It is backed by a short cave of phreatic origin. The rising just upstream was once pumped for a farm water supply.

The next significant feature is Lover's

Figure 32: Reynards Cave, Dovedale
photo: Tony Waltham

experiments have shown that they are fed by streams sinking in the Swinscoe, Weaver Hills and Cauldon Low areas.

Just before the footbridge there is the Hamps Spring **9**. This is an overflow from the Ilam Upper Rising and is fed entirely by the River Hamps sink at Waterhouses.

Cross the footbridge and follow the path across the fields to Rushley. Follow the road right and shortly after re-crossing the River take the path left, which leads diagonally across the valley floor and thence via Castern Hall and Castern Farms back up the hillside to Stanshope. Above Castern Farm you will pass through an interesting area of minor reef knolls, the eroded remains of mud mounds. These originated as mounds of fine shell debris bound together by algae on the seabed. They were previously confused with the marginal reef structures (as in lower Dovedale), but these ones do not mark the edge of the early Carboniferous carbonate platform.

Figure 33: Dovedale at its most dramatic
where the River has cut a deep gorge between two Reef Knolls   *photo: Tony Waltham*

EXCURSION 7:
THE MANIFOLD/HAMPS VALLEYS
Distance: 17 or 27-30km

Quite apart from being a beautiful limestone valley, in many ways a slightly scaled down neighbour of the nearby Dove *see Excursion 6,* the Manifold taken together with the Hamps, is also somewhat special in that it had a light railway line engineered through it in the 1890s. This was the Leek & Manifold Valley Light Railway (L&MVLR). It was just 2'6" track gauge and ran from its 'full-standard' connection at Waterhouses, down the Hamps and then all the way up the Manifold to the final terminus at Hulme End. A candidate for the title of "railway line with the greatest speleological interest in Britain", it even had a station called Thor's Cave and Wetton.

As a passenger-carrying/tourist feature it was almost 100 years ahead of its time; never a financial success, it closed in 1934. Most of the upper section from near Wetton to Hulme End was made into a public highway, but the lower section, right through to Waterhouses is now a dedicated cycle track. As such it traverses one of the most beautiful sections of countryside of any such route in Britain. Regrettably, the lower section of the Manifold valley between the Hamps junction and Rushley has no public right of way along it, and is not Access Land.

At times of low to medium flow the River Manifold sinks at Wetton Mill, some 4km after crossing onto the limestone just below Hulme End, and resurges close to the point where it flows off the limestone at Ilam *see Excursion 6.* In wetter weather the final sink points migrate downstream until there is a continuous surface flow. In the past, several attempts have been made to induce a permanent surface flow by the blocking of sinks with concrete plugs. These have all been unsuccessful but the plugs provide useful markers for the sinks. The Manifold is unique amongst Peak District rivers in that several segments of an active stream-cave system have been explored at depths of up to 40m below the river bed. They are, of course, liable to rapid flooding following rainfall.

We will assume here that you are taking this as a cycle ride all the way from Hulme End to Waterhouses. Although there are many small meanderings and tight bends, it is basically a linear route. If you have two vehicles then it can be just that, but otherwise a little more energy must be reserved for the return journey (see below).

SUGGESTED STARTING POINTS

From the public car park **1** near Hulme End, just off the B5054, follow the route signed "Manifold Way" down-valley. The river soon crosses onto the limestone, but it is a further 4km before it sinks at Wetton Mill **2**.

After 1km the now overgrown remains of the once very productive Ecton Hill Copper Mines can be seen across the river to the left. These were extensive and continue for some distance. From just before the tunnel and Ecton Bridge there is an alternative route on the opposite side of the river, but this is primarily a pedestrian route.

At Wetton Mill there is another public car park and toilets, and it is thus an alternative starting point **2**. From here Nan Tor Cave **3**, is just across the River Manifold, in the side of the Nan Tor reef knoll, which is riddled with relict phreatic cave passages. Excavation of a rock shelter on the north side has revealed a late glacial to Iron Age sequence of deposits.

The first major sinks of the River Manifold are around 100m south of the Mill. **4**. Wetton Mill Sink takes the most water but is thought to be a large and so far impenetrable boulder choke. The choke has been by-passed by Darfar Pot, whose entrance is in the crag a few metres east of the main sink. Over 365m of passage have been explored in a three-dimensional, joint-guided complex that descends over 40m beneath the river bed. The nearby Darfar Crag Swallet was probably descended in the 1920s but subsequently became filled with debris and is still being re-excavated. Riverside Swallet (Pot) some 20m downstream of the main sink area is 10m deep and has about 65m of passage.

Some 1.5km downstream from Wetton Mill there is a complex pattern of sinks known collectively as Redhurst Swallet **5**. There is only one major cave here, entered by a small joint-guided passage at the base of a reef limestone cliff. The 300m of joint-aligned phreatic passages are almost entirely below river level and extremely flood prone. Ossom's Crag Cave and Ossom's Eyrie are short relict phreatic passages high in the reef above. On the next left bend of the river T-Pot and Wednesday Pot **6** are to be found. These were first entered in 1980 and are clearly part of the same system. T-Pot has its entrance in a large concrete plug in the river bed, and has over 200m of explored passage, whereas Wednesday Pot has about 50m.

Close to the next left bend there is Ladyside Pot **7**. This is another tight vertical joint, but sufficiently far downstream to function as an estavelle discharging water under certain flood conditions and accepting an inflow at others. Some 460m of passage have been explored to a maximum depth of 21m beneath the river bed. There are two downstream and four upstream sumps, two of which are complex. High above these on the opposite side of the river is the prominent entrance to Thor's Cave **8**, an ancient phreatic remnant cave in a large reef-limestone crag located just over 1km southwest of Wetton village. Excavation has yielded animal and human remains dating from

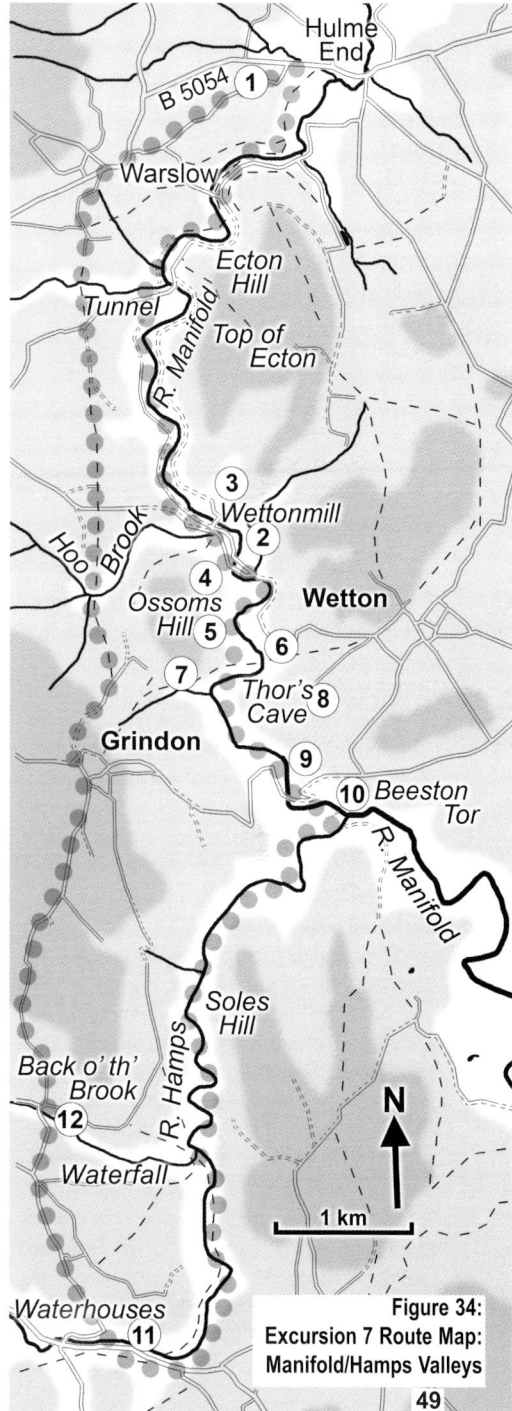

Figure 34: Excursion 7 Route Map: Manifold/Hamps Valleys

49

Figure 35: "Thor's Cave and Wetton" station, on the L&MVLR (c. 1910) photo: courtesy Lindsey Porter see box p.48

Pleistocene to Romano-British times. Elderbush Cave, just around the hill to the south and 100m above the valley floor, has yielded stalagmites dated to over 1.7 million years ago, demonstrating that the cave had been drained even by then. On the next bend of the river, just before the road bridge, is the Weags Bridge Resurgence **9**. Like Ladyside Pot this is an estavelle, which acts as both a sink and a rising depending on the hydrological conditions. There are about 21m of accessible passage here.

Continue downstream to the junction of the Manifold with the River Hamps which may be dry indicating that all the flow is sinking upstream. Downstream is the impressive Beeston Tor, the next reef knoll down from the crag that contains Thor's and Elderbush Caves **10**. Beeston Tor contains seven separate cave entrances, the most famous, at river level, leading to St Bertram's Cave, where a Saxon coin hoard was found. A 9m climb up a rift leads to another entrance higher in the Tor, Jackdaw's Hole.

The Manifold Way continues up the Hamps valley towards Waterhouses **11**,

passing the small entrance to Hamps Valley Cave. The Hell Holes Sinks are located between the 6th and 7th bridges upstream from the confluence with the Manifold. They are only active when sinks further upstream are overtopped but it is clear that they can accommodate a large flow of water as the river bed is notably lower upstream. About 500m upstream of the sinks there is a large tributary valley from the west. This carries the Breedon Brook during extended wet periods but is dry for most of the year, the water sinking at Back o' the Brook **12** from where it takes a more direct underground route to the Ilam risings. From the Breedon Brook confluence continue up the Hamps valley to Waterhouses where the river sinks.

There is a relatively direct and substantially off-road route from Waterhouses via Waterfall, Grindon and Warslow back to Hulme End, with short-cuts back to Wetton Mill, or to Hulme End avoiding Warslow and the B5053 completely – total trip distances being 27 and 30km (or 17km for the Wetton Mill start).

---- ---- ~~ ---- ----

EXCURSION 8: UPPER LATHKILLDALE WALK: approx.11km

The Upper Lathkill, from near Monyash to Over Haddon, is one of the most beautiful valleys of the White Peak. Along with four other nearby dales it forms an integral part of the Derbyshire Dales National Nature Reserve (NNR). A central section of the River Lathkill is also included in the Lathkill and Mandale Mines Scheduled Ancient Monument designation.

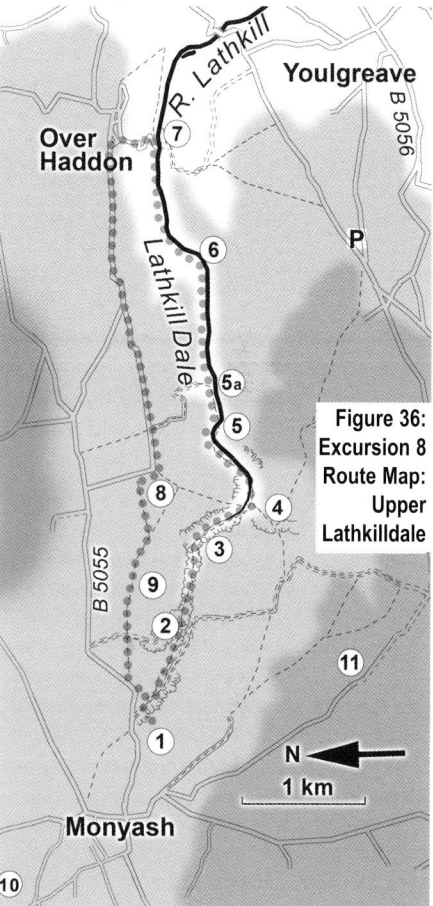

Figure 36: Excursion 8 Route Map: Upper Lathkilldale

An ideal starting point is Monyash Village 1, where there is a Public House, the Bull's Head, a café and a village shop. Roadside car parking is available about 300m from Monyash along the Bakewell road and there are public toilets at this point. The Public Car Park at Over Haddon provides an alternative starting point.

The centre of Monyash is situated on a tiny outlier of dark mudstone of uncertain age. These are surrounded by the Eyam Limestone Formation roughly in the centre of a shallow structural basin in the lagoonal part of the Derbyshire massif. The basin is fringed by small reef mounds, also belonging to the Eyam Limestone. The catchment for the River Lathkill extends to the northwest as far as Chelmorton and is distinguished from the other limestone catchments in the Peak District by having no allogenic stream inputs (streams flowing from the Millstone Grit). Thus the Lathkill discharges only accumulated percolation water.

The flow of water in the valley has been impacted by two lead-mine drainage soughs, Magpie and Lathkill Dale. Magpie Sough, which lies to the northeast of Monyash and discharges into the River Wye *see pages 16 and 43,* has captured drainage that would otherwise have targeted Lathkill Dale. Prior to the driving of the sough it seems likely that the Lathkill had its source nearer to the village, but the upper 3km of the valley to just above Lathkill Head Cave are now perennially dry and flows below this point are lower than would have been the case under natural conditions. Lathkill Dale Sough is lower down the valley and runs beneath the river channel for part of its course. Water leaks into the sough throughout the year but during the summer low-flow period the entire flow is absorbed and the surface channel dries up. Permanent surface flow does not start until Bubble Springs, below Over Haddon.

Figure 37: The usually dry section of Upper Lathkill Dale, above Lathkill Head Cave. Note the ancient screes in the foreground   *photo: Tony Waltham*

There are several caves in the area and although none are of any great extent (Lathkill Head Cave is the longest at 1800m) they have a reputation as being amongst the most strenuous in Derbyshire, with extensive very low crawls.

From the Monyash parking area take the footpath down-valley to the southeast. After about 900m a small dry valley, Ricklow Dale, enters from the left. Ricklow Cave **2**, has a small entrance at the base of a cliff on the north side of the valley. The entrance was mined but it leads to natural passages and excavation of sediment has opened a connection beneath the valley floor to Lathkill Head Cave. The nearby Ricklow Marble Quarry yielded building stone and ornamental "figured marble" from beds flanking a mud-mound. The rock contains many fossil crinoid stem fragments and "Gigantoproductid" shells and is known as marble because it takes a polish, even though it is not actually a metamorphosed limestone.

Just before the valley starts to make a sweep to the right you will come upon the impressive main entrance to Lathkill Head Cave **3**. This cave system as a whole is an excellent example of epiphreatic development along prominent bedding planes in the lagoonal facies of the Monsal Dale Limestone. The main passage is wide but low with extensive banks of coarse sediment. Still active, it fills to the roof in wet weather, but two dry routes into the cave have been excavated from the plateau above the valley. The 'Top Entrance' leads into two large chambers, the Waiting Room and Lathkiller Hall, and the 'Garden Path Entrance' leads into the Dream Time Chamber. All three chambers contain fine speleothems and extensive breakdown. Downstream, the cave trends towards Cales Dale Cave **4**, and a hydrological connection has been proved both by dye tracing and by the presence in Cales Dale Cave of shredded wetsuit fragments, washed down from Lathkill Head Cave. However, the intervening passage is too low and constricted for human access

The small entrance to Critchlow Cave is almost opposite Lathkill Head Cave and was once thought to be a downstream continuation of the Lathkill system that had been dissected by surface drainage. However, it now seems that although the two caves are on the same inception horizon they grew independently.

At about 2km from the road the main valley starts a large sweep to the left and a much more substantial tributary valley, Cales Dale, joins from the south. About 150m up this side valley there are three cave entrances close together, the Cales Dale Caves **4**. The most extensive is Lower Cales Dale Cave, just below the path, which contains over 1050m of passage, most of which can only be explored under drought conditions. Cales Dale New Cave has its entrance almost opposite Lower Cales Dale Cave and the entrance to Upper Cales Dale Cave is a few metres away. Both are relict systems, the Upper Cave being a phreatic tube blocked after some 60m and the New Cave a low bedding tube that becomes too low to penetrate after about 20m

Below the Cales Dale junction the Lathkill Valley is deeply incised into the plateau surface and displays fine buttresses footed by screes, which mask any cave entrances that might be present there. Some of the screes are cemented and probably formed under periglacial conditions, but others are still active.

About 800m downstream of Cales Dale the river flows over a prominent tufa waterfall **5**, and in drought conditions some 60m of cave has been explored within the tufa (Lathkill Resurgence Cave). The waterfall is an artificial feature formed through the quarrying of these extensive tufa deposits. The tufa deposits are a result of chemical and biochemical processes, but present day deposition rates do not account for their considerable extent and they most probably started to accumulate during a warmer interglacial period.

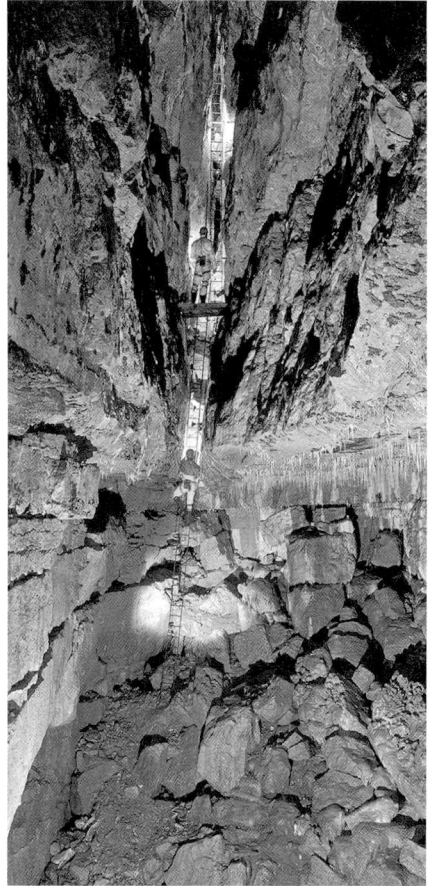

Figure 38: The Garden Path, Lathkill Head Cave photo: Paul Deakin

About 300m downstream of the waterfall Calling Low Dale is a tributary from the right (south) and opposite this is another unnamed tributary valley from the north. A ruined building at the bottom of the dale **5a** is the former Carter's Corn Mill and the run-in tail of Smallpenny Sough is vaguely visible next to a ruined lead miners' coe (a small stone shed). For those who would like to shorten the walk, a public footpath leads up the unnamed dale to Haddon Grove **8** from where a footpath can be followed back to Monyash.

Figure 39: Water Icicle Close Cavern   *photo: Paul Deakin*

on a stainless steel ladder and wind a hand generator to illuminate the lower shaft where the disk-engine was located.

A little further along the Dale you pass between the pillars of a former aqueduct that conveyed water from a leat across the valley to power a water wheel at Mandale Mine. The tail of Mandale Sough is immediately to the right of the path and on the left side the surface remains of former mine buildings can be explored.

After Mandale Mine there are a series of weirs and fishing ponds before reaching an old mill **7** and the steep narrow lane on the left that leads to Over Haddon village with its public car park and Pub, The Lathkill Hotel (once The Miners Arms). However, before heading up the lane continue down the valley for a further 200m to view Bubble Springs, the perennial source of the River Lathkill.

From Over Haddon you can either retrace your steps back to Monyash, or from the village there is a shorter and quicker route first along the road heading west, and then just past Haddon Grove Farm **8**, take the footpath across the fields. This takes you close to the ancient tumulus (burial chamber) of Ringham Low **9**.

There are two further important features in this area, not taken in by this walk, but of considerable interest. The first of these is the Hillocks and Knotlow mines area **10** some 1.5km northwest of Monyash. These adjacent and connected lead mines have both intersected natural cave passages including bedding-plane-guided phreatic tubes. Hillocks Mine is partly in a series of pipe veins that are palaeokarstic features.

Continuing down-valley from Carters Mill the large Cowgate Pool weir marks the start of the stretch of channel along which flow is lost to Lathkill Sough and depending on the time of year and weather conditions you might notice that the flow of the river gradually decreases downstream and can cease completely. About 900m below the weir the valley briefly heads north and a bridge on the right provides access to the ruin of Bateman's House **6**. This is thought to have been a mine manager, or agent's house, built by the Lathkill Dale Lead Mining Company around 1825. It certainly became the mine office and control point for up to 120 miners in the 1820 to 1830 period but it also held a secret. It was built in order to cover the tops of two stone lined shafts within which a novel water-powered engine was constructed. This was a 10ft diameter tilting-disk device which used the weight of water run into it to create circular motion via a concentric shaft. The power thus derived was then used to pump water from the mines beneath. Water had always been a problem in the mines that crossed beneath the Dale. You can now climb down the surface shaft

Knotlow Cavern is a natural cave system that has been intersected, and heavily modified, by lead miners. There are three shaft entrances, two descending vertically for 65m and a third with three shorter pitches. All the shafts lead to a streamway and this water has been traced to the Lathkill as well as to Magpie Sough, confirming that the sough has captured some of the natural drainage of Lathkill Dale.

The second feature is Water Icicle Close Cavern **11**, one of the more unusual cave systems in the area. A small diameter, 32m-deep, mine shaft (now securely lidded), hand-picked through solid limestone, enters the roof of a natural chamber formed at the junction of three large phreatic tubes. Each of these is blocked by fill after about 100 to 200m. Speleothems from the cave have been dated and found to be over 350,000 years old and the cave system, which pre-dates local valley incision, was probably developed in the early Pleistocene. It is likely to be a fragment of an extensive but as yet undiscovered cave system. The speleothems that remain are relics of a stalagmite mining operation to provide "spar" for a grotto at Chatsworth House. Whilst its chance discovery and location are interesting, this site lies on private land and there is nothing to see on the surface.

EXCURSION 9: THE MATLOCK AREA

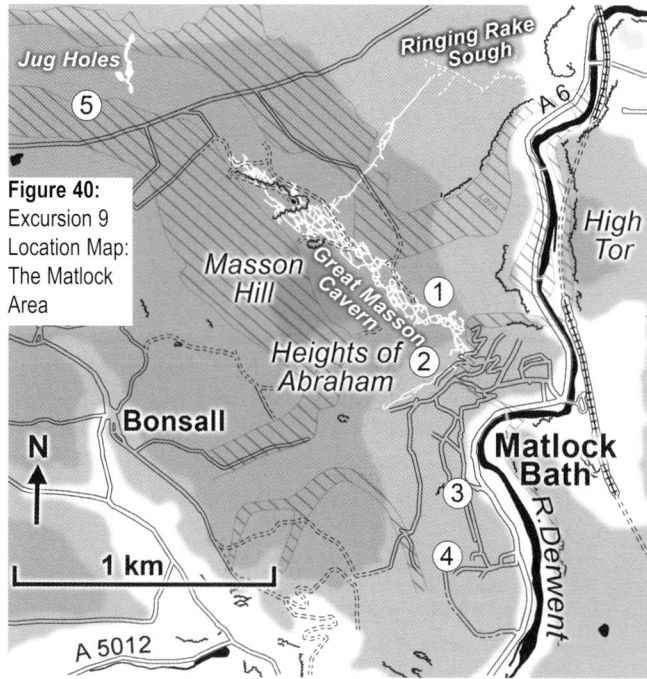

Figure 40: Excursion 9 Location Map: The Matlock Area

MASSON HILL CAVES and MINES

This is one of the most complex suites of caves and abandoned metalliferous mines in Britain.

The caves both pre-date and post-date the late Carboniferous mineralization of the Derbyshire Dome and they are important as they provide insights into the understanding of vein-guided karst drainage elsewhere in the Peak District. They were abandoned by flowing water over one hundred thousand years ago following incision of the Derwent Valley and act as 'natural museums' preserving some of the earliest Pleistocene glacial deposits in Britain.

There are now many public attractions in and around the Matlock–Matlock Bath area, including museums, show caves, show mines and a cable car. The main railway line, originally a central portion of the London Midland and Scottish (LMS) Railways direct London to Manchester line but abandoned beyond Matlock since the 1960s, was forced into three tunnels between Cromford and Matlock stations. Although the mainline railway now ends at

Figure 41: Great Masson Cavern *photo: Paul Deakin*

Matlock, and "Matlock Riverside Station", is the southern terminal of the Peak Railway that is run by steam locomotive enthusiasts.

The area has a complex and fascinating geological history, and a rich mining and industrial heritage that was recognised in 2002 when part of the area was inscribed on the UNESCO Cultural World Heritage list. It is a busy and complex area, made all the more so by its topography. For all of these reasons we are not suggesting a fixed circular tour, but merely signposting what we regard as the speleologically and mineralogically interesting features of the area.

The River Derwent flows southwards through a major gorge cut across the Masson anticline on the eastern flank of the limestone massif between Matlock and Cromford. The gorge's situation is anomalous in that it slices through both limestones and lavas in an eastward-plunging anticlinal fold, when a route of apparent less resistance would have been along the shale outcrop only a kilometre to the east. A series of high reef limestone masses as seen in High Tor appear to have trapped the river as it was superimposed from the shales on to the limestone.

To the west of the gorge lies Masson Hill, where inclined limestones contain two lava flows, each about 20m thick, and several ash layers up to 30cm thick. Locally these relatively impermeable layers have influenced the movement of underground fluids, particularly when magnesium-rich solutions were introduced as an early phase of mineralization yielding an extensive tract of dolomite on the summit of Masson Hill.

This combination of limestones, dolomites, lavas, clay wayboards (ash layers), and mineralization is breached by a complex of caves. These are, in the main, phreatic passages, formed particularly along the dolomite/limestone boundary. Though not very extensive, these caves were penetrated by the old lead miners in several places and some of the resultant mine-cum-cave systems have been developed as tourist attractions. There is little vadose modification of the caves but the throughput of water might have contributed to the erosion of the gorge.

Warm springs (20°C) rise at Matlock Bath – once a health spa – and deposit sheets of tufa, particularly around the Pavilion and the New Bath Hotel. Objects placed in the water of the "Petrifying Well" are coated with a film of tufa in about 10 years.

1 GREAT MASSON CAVERN

The entrance to this tourist cave/mine is along a worked-out mineral vein oriented west–east, but a short distance inside it encounters a series of phreatic dissolution caverns trending obliquely up-dip towards the northwest. At least some of the phreatic dissolution occurred during a phase of mid-Carboniferous palaeokarstification. This breached numerous pipe-vein cavities, variously lined with calcite, fluorspar and galena. Although largely worked out by the old miners, some at the northern end of Masson Cavern still retain their calcite fills. Renewed phreatic dissolution occurred in Pleistocene times before the gorge was incised. Traces of a former fill of glacial outwash sands, silts and gravels can be seen in Great Masson Cavern, though the fill is much better displayed beyond the tourist route in the old workings of Black Ox and High Loft mines. Thus the Great Masson Cavern represents a combination of a mid-Carboniferous palaeokarst, late Carboniferous hydrothermal karst, Pleistocene phreatic dissolution caves, and various fills of glacial meltwater outwash sediments – a complex story.

Gentlewomen's Pipe was formerly connected to the upper end of Masson Mine, but fluorspar quarrying has destroyed the connection. It can now be entered via Ringing Rake Sough (also known as Youd's Level) in the valley bottom. The Jant Mine sector has a cavern with a fill of glacial outwash sediments that show a magnetic reversal, dating their emplacement at more than 780,000 years ago.

2 RUTLAND CAVERN

A little lower down the Masson hillside, this show cave/mine was also entered by miners. The entrance tunnel cuts through one of the lava flows and the caverns beyond are also a complex blend of ancient palaeokarst, hydrothermal karst and early Pleistocene dissolution activity.

3 TEMPLE MINE

Near the foot of the hillside, this is a short fluorspar mine of the 1920s, now open to visitors. The mine also intersected caverns partly infilled by Pleistocene sediments.

4 ROYAL MINE

Above Temple Mine and Gulliver's Kingdom another mine-cum-cave complex was at one time open as a show cave although not operating at the time of writing [2009]. Formerly part of the Hopping and Tear Breeches mines it was last worked for fluorspar in the 1950s. Pipe veins and cavities as well as replacement ore bodies of fluorspar in dolomite again incorporate sediment-filled caves similar to Temple Mine.

5 JUG HOLES

On the north side of Masson Hill a large natural entrance leads to a network of partly collapsed lead and fluorspar workings. A short shaft and passages leading west extend into a series of natural chambers developed where the limestone rests on deeply weathered basaltic lava, both being inclined to the north. The lava is now in the form of greenish clay largely covered with a slope of stalagmite bosses. A separate series of caverns extends downhill, with much clay fill that is thought to be composed of derived loess.

Three Derbyshire Caving Association publications in their Cave + Mine Conservation Audit Series cover the Matlock area in considerable detail, *see box p.64.*

EXCURSION 10: THE BRASSINGTON AREA
Walk or Cycle Ride: 6.5km or 9km

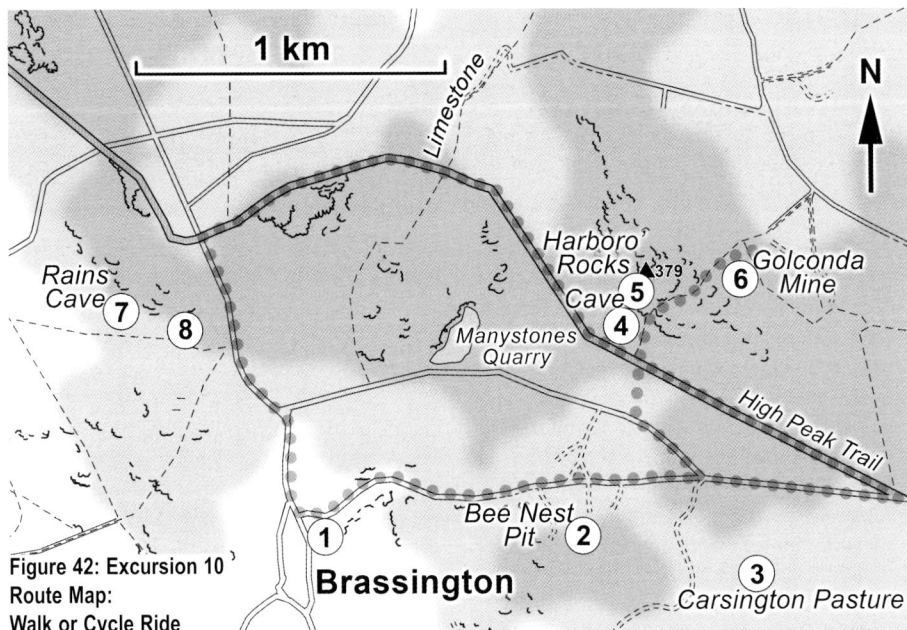

Figure 42: Excursion 10
Route Map:
Walk or Cycle Ride

This short circular walk or cycle ride assumes a start from in or near the village of Brassington 1, and features are based on this and numbered anti-clockwise.

Near the southern margin of the White Peak, some 6km westsouthwest of Matlock Bath, above the village of Brassington, the limestones have locally been altered to dolomite. There are also silica sand "pockets", the craggy escarpment of Harborough Rocks 5 and several isolated dolomite tors. The latter resulted from erosional disaggregation of partly dolomitized limestones being followed by removal of the dolosand debris by sludging under frozen ground conditions, leaving upstanding cores, or tors.

To the south of Harborough Rocks several sand pockets have been worked for refractory sands. Sands, gravels and clays of

Miocene-Pliocene age, known as the Brassington Formation, are exposed in several pits e.g. Bee Nest Pit 2. There are other sand-filled pockets in the fields to the north and west, as well as on Carsington Pasture 3, and Wester Hollow to the southeast. Relics of a former cover of Millstone Grit Group shales and an insoluble residue of chert nodules have been found in some pits, indicating a complex early karstic history, and plant fossils of Late-Miocene age have been found in the youngest clays of the Bees Nest Pit. The sands were probably derived from an escarpment of Triassic rocks as it retreated to the south. Once a continuous sheet over the southern White Peak, the sands and clays sagged into large dissolution collapse pits in early Pleistocene times owing to karstic water levels being lowered

Figure 43: Harborough Rocks *photo: David Judson*

as the major valleys started to incise.

Golconda Mine **6**, was entered in the 18th century by a 130m-deep shaft that is now hidden amongst the mill buildings east of Harborough Rocks. Part of the shaft intersected a narrow vertical natural cavern. A complex of some 5km of mine workings also broke into several large "shacks", dissolution and collapse caverns that were developed at the dolomite/limestone contact about 130m below the present surface. Disaggregation of partly dolomitized limestone and its subsequent removal led to the formation of caverns up to 100m long. Mineral pipe-veins also occur at this level and in parts of the mine-cum-cave system collapse has allowed some of the sands of the Brassington Formation to wash down into the caverns.

With an entrance clearly visible in the escarpment, Harborough Rocks Cave **4**, is one of several archaeological caves in the area that have yielded Neolithic and Romano-British remains. According to Daniel Defoe, a miner's family lived in one such cave in the early 18th century.

Carsington Pasture **3**, to the southeast of Harborough Rocks, has several small caves, some of archaeological significance. Rains Cave **7**, is an incompletely excavated archaeological cave in the east end of Longcliffe Crags, a few metres west of the old Observer Corps building **8**.

---- ---- ~~~ ---- ----

Figure 44: Manystones Quarry, Brassington: photo T D Ford.

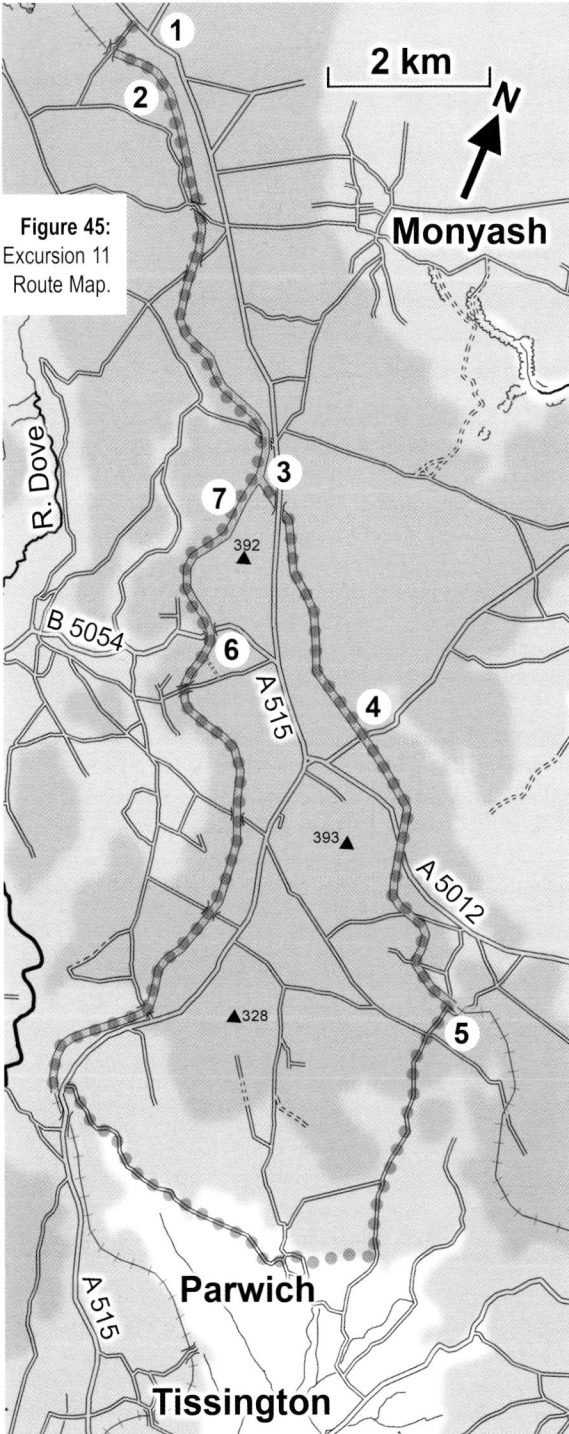

2 km

N

Monyash

Figure 45:
Excursion 11
Route Map.

R. Dove

B 5054

392 ▲

A 515

393 ▲

A 5012

▲ 328

A 515

Parwich

Tissington

EXCURSION 11:
THE HIGH PEAK and
TISSINGTON TRAILS

Cycle Ride:
about 40km

The suggested starting point is just off the A515 Buxton-Ashbourne road about 500m west of Pomeroy **1**. The start of the "Pippenwell Road" presents a handy parking spot. From there go along the A515 for a few metres towards Buxton to where a wide but rough short section of bridle-way connects with National Cycle Network 68, (here also the Pennine Bridleway), see p.63. Here the route follows the former Buxton to Ashbourne railway, itself constructed over the line of an earlier horse drawn tramway, but with extra cuttings and embankments smoothing out the somewhat angular route of the former. For the next 1.7km to Sparklow the old line can still be traced running to the west of Hurdlow Town and east of Cronkston Low **2**.

At the fork of the ways **3**, near Parsley Hay and shortly after the cafe and cycle hire centre, take the left hand "High Peak Trail", which follows the trackbed of the early mineral tramway, The Cromford and High Peak Mineral Railway (CHPMR) – a relict from the hey-day of canals. This was a precursor of the modern railway

THE LIMESTONE WAY

Created in the 1990s, this is a long distance footpath, of 80km total length. It starts from a connection with the Heart of England Way (Cannock Chase to Bourton-on-the-Water 160km) near Rocester, in Staffordshire, some way from any limestone. The path follows the valley of the Dove, crossing into limestone country near Thorpe, from where it leaves Dovedale and goes cross-country by way of Tissington, Parwich, Brassington and Grange Mill to Upper Town near Matlock Bath. From there a spur goes to Matlock itself and the main route runs north past Winster and through Youlgreave, Monyash and Flagg. It crosses the Monsal Trail in Miller's Dale and then goes by way of Wheston and Hurd Low to end in Castleton. At Hurd Low it passes close to one of the most spectacular features of the Derbyshire underground, the Titan Shaft *see Figure 15 on page 25 and Front Cover photograph* and ends close to another one, the Peak Cavern Gorge and Peak Cavern (The Devil's Arse in the Peak) itself.

For the most part this is only a footpath, although isolated sections in the south and the northern portion (19km) from Flagg to Castleton do follow bridleways, quiet roads or tracks. Throughout it traverses some fine limestone terrain, right through the heart of the White Peak of the Peak District.

In the context of this booklet the Limestone Way is utilised by Excursion (Cycle Ride) 2 down Cave Dale into Castleton, and met with again on Excursions 10 and 11 near Brassington.

---

network, connecting the Peak Forest Canal near Whaley Bridge in the north with the Cromford Canal in the east. It was a horse drawn tramway with short-section cast-iron rails laid directly on stone sleepers. Steam powered beam-engines operated winding drums at the head of long inclines near each end. It connected the extensive canal network of the Manchester basin with the canals of the Nottingham-Derby-Trent network. Started in 1825 but not fully opened until 1831 it was rather late for this sort of development.

At about 3.5km from the Parsley Hay junction you pass Friden brickworks **4**, where refractory bricks are manufactured. This is located here due to the presence of pocket deposits containing silica sand see *p.58*, although all raw materials are now imported.

Leave the Cycleway at the picnic point where it crosses Parwich Lane (8km from Parsley Hay) **5**. Follow this lane (south) into the village where there is a public house, the Sycamore Inn.

From Parwich follow the road west through Alsop en le Dale. Shortly after the village a footpath runs west and connects with Route 68, here called the "Tissington Trail". Cyclists need to continue along the lane and join Route 68 from the A515.

Follow the Tissington Trail north past Johnson's Knoll, a fine example of a knoll reef. A little further north is the old Hartington Station **6**, where there is a short walk around Hartington Meadows, a Derbyshire Wildlife Trust site which contains a sand pit and pocket deposits. Continuing north the trail passes through two cuttings **7**, with good sections of dolomitized limestone, *see also Figure 44, Excursion 10.*

FURTHER READING/BIBLIOGRAPHY

There is a wealth of literature on the caves of this area and their exploration in the journals of the various caving clubs, mostly with somewhat limited availability. The following articles and books should be available through most public libraries, or by prior arrangement, through the BCRA or larger/longer established caving club libraries. The BCRA National Caving Library has recently been re-established and greatly improved and is now located at Glutton Bridge, just within Derbyshire and near the starting/finishing point for Excursion 11 and NCN 68 (NGR 084 667).

BECK J S 1975 The Caves of the Foolow-Eyam-Stoney Middleton Area, Derbyshire, and Their Genesis. *Trans.BCRA 2,* 1-11.

BISHOP M J 1982 The Cave Hunters. Buxton: Derbyshire Museum Service.

BRAMWELL D 1977 *Archaeology & Palaeontology.* In Ford, T D. (ed.) *Limestones and Caves of the Peak District.* Norwich: Geo Books pp.263-91.

BRANIGAN K, & DEARNE M J 1991 *A Gazetteer of Romano-British Cave Sites and their Finds.* Department of Archaeology & Prehistory, Sheffield University.

CHRISTOPHER N S J, CRABTREE R W, & CULSHAW S M 1981 A Hydrological Study of the Castleton Area. *Trans. BCRA 8,* 189-206.

DALTON R, FOX H, & JONES P 1988 *Classical Landforms of the White Peak.* Classical Landforms Guide 9, Geographical Assoc, Sheffield, 48pp (2nded.1999).

DAWKINS W B 1874 *Cave Hunting: Researches on the Evidence of Caves Respecting the Early Inhabitants of Europe.* London: Macmillan.

FLINDALL R, SWAINN J, & HAYES A 1981 A Survey of the Masson Cave-cum-mine Complex, Matlock. *Bull.of the Peak District Mines Historical Soc.8,* 103-8.

FORD T D 1963 The Dolomite Tors of Derbyshire. *E Midlands Geographer 3* (19), 148-53.

------------1977 *Limestones and Caves of the Peak District.* Geo Books, Norwich, 469p.

------------ 1986 The Evolution of the Castleton Cave Systems, Derbyshire. *Cave Science 13,* 131-48.

------------ 1987 The Origin of the Winnats Pass, Castleton, Derbyshire. *Mercian Geologist 10*(4), 241-9.

------------ 1996 *The Castleton Area.* Geologists Association Guide 56, 96p.

------------ 1997 The Development of the Derwent Gorge and its Caves, Matlock, Derbyshire - a review. *Cave & Karst Science 24*(1), 5-19.

------------ 2000 Vein Cavities: the early evolution of the Castleton Cave Systems. *Cave & Karst Science 27,* 5-14.

------------ 2002 *Rocks & Scenery of the Peak District.* Landmark Pub'ing, Ashbourne, 96p.

------------ 2002 The Geology of the Matlock Mines - a review. Mining History 14(6), 1-34.

------------ 2005 *Derbyshire Blue John.* Ashbourne Editions (Landmark Publishing), Ashbourne, 2nded, 112p.

------------ 2008 *Castleton Caves.* Landmark Publishing, Ashbourne, 96p.

------------ BUREK C V, & BECK J S 1975 The Evolution of Bradwell Dale & its Caves. *Trans.BCRA 2,* 133-40.

------------ GASCOYNE M, & BECK J S 1983 Speleothem Dates & Pleistocene Chronology in the Peak District of Derbyshire. *Cave Science 10,* 103-15.

----------- 1996 Speleogenesis: the Evolution of the Castleton Caves. *Geology Today 12* (3), 101-9.

----------- and KING R J 1966 The Golconda Caverns, Brassington, Derbyshire. Trans. CRG 7, 1-14.

----------- and RIEUWERTS J H 2000 Lead Mining in the Peak. 4[th]ed. Peak District Mines Historical Society, Matlock, 208p.

GUNN J 1991 Water Tracing Experiments in the Castleton Karst 1950-90. *Trans. BCRA 18,* 43-6.

---------- 2004 Encyclopedia of Caves & Karst Science, Fitzroy Dearborn (especially p.575-8, Peak District, England.

JACKSON J W 1962 *Archaeology and Palaeontology.* In Cullingford, CHD (ed.) *British Caving (2nd edition).* Routledge, 252-346.

MARSDEN A et al 1991 Peak and Speedwell Cave Systems - Exploration & Science. *Cave Science 18,* 1-58.

PITTY A F 1968 The Scale and Significance of Solutional loss from the limestone tract of the southern Pennines. *Proc.Geologists Assoc. 79,* 153-78.

PORTER L 2002 *The Leek & Manifold Valley Light Railway,* Ashbourne Editions, Ashbourne, 96p.

ROBEY J A 1965 The Drainage of the Area between the River Wye and the River Lathkill. *Proc.BSA 3,* 1-10.

WALSH P T, BOULTER M C, IJTABA M & URBANI D M 1972 The Preservation of the Neogene Brassington Formation of the Southern Pennines and its Bearing on the Evolution of Upland Britain. *Jour.Geol. Soc, London 128,* 519-59.

WALTHAM A C, SIMMS M J, FARRANT A R, & GOLDIE H S 1997 *Karst & Caves of Great Britain.* Chapman & Hall, London (for the JNCC, Peterborough), 358p.

WORLEY N E & NASH D 1977 The Geological Evolution of the Jug Holes Caves, Matlock. *Trans.BCRA 4,* 381-401.

THE PENNINE BRIDLEWAY

This is the first "purpose-built" long distance bridleway for horse riders, mountain-bikers and walkers in Britain. It is also the first to include two significant circular sections – the 76km Mary Towneley Loop in Lancashire and the Settle Loop in Yorkshire. When complete, it will run from Middleton Top, near Middleton-by-Wirksworth (recommended cyclists start), or Hartington (for horse riders) all the way to Berwick upon Tweed in Northumberland – about 560km although in reality only 20% of it is actually off-road. The southern third across Derbyshire and on into Greater Manchester, Lancashire and Yorkshire is now complete, including the two loops.

This bridleway uses the High Peak Trail (or the Tissington Trail) to Pomeroy, the starting point for Ride 11 *see p.60,* and then heads north, crossing Wye Dale at its junction with Great Rocks Dale, through Wheston and on to Peak Forest and Hayfield to leave Derbyshire for Greater Manchester and the Dark Peak near Hadfield.

This is a most excellent and welcome effort on the part of the local authorities and the three National Parks, Peak District, Yorkshire Dales and Northumberland that have sponsored it. Although The Pennine Bridleway follows the same route as National Cycle Network (NCN) route 68 along some sections, it is not the same entity and has very different end points. This can be a little confusing!